Praise and Endo
Memoirs of Jose

When I first read excerpts of the José Lopez Lopez memoirs on the web, I was drawn to the firsthand look at what my grandparents and so many others experienced in their saga from Spain to Hawaii and beyond. José's descendants are so very fortunate to have this amazing history.

Because my grandparents were also on a plantation near Hilo, I was especially interested, and as I read the recollections of José, I saw my grandmother's brothers' names. From our own family history, I realized that José's father, who had come to Hawaii in 1907 and cleared the unused hillside for sugar cane, had probably sold or given the rights to that hillside to my great grandfather when José's family left for the mainland. My great grandfather and his sons carried on the work that José and his father had begun, enabling my family to save money and continue on to California. My family's success is directly related to José's family efforts.

We are the fortunate benefactors of the hardworking immigrants that came before us, and I am so grateful to Susan for sharing her family's history. José's words bring to life the family stories we have heard.

- STEVE ALONZO
"Hawaiian Spaniards" Facebook page Administrator

The stories of the Spanish immigrants that came through Hawaii 1907-1913 are so very similar even though each family is unique. José's story is very familiar to my grandparents since they also came over on the Heliopolis, migrated to northern California and worked up and down the state harvesting fruits and vegetables. I am sure that our families crossed paths many times - the names mentioned are ones that I am familiar with. José's family is very fortunate that he wrote his memories down. For most of us, we only have the remnants of oral stories that we heard and that were changed throughout the years. This story should and will be cherished by the family.

-GLORIA LOPEZ,
Author: *AN AMERICAN PAELLA*
Becoming American While Staying Spanish:
A Century of Memories in Winters, CA

I love the inclusion of personal photos and other inserts to enhance references made by José Lopez. Nicely done. Thank you for publishing this work of our grandfather. It is quite obviously a labor of love and you have done a wonderful job.

- JERRY HASSINGER
Grandson of Joseph Lopez Lopez

It is essential that these stories are known and not forgotten. Most importantly, let coming generations know their roots and value what their ancestors suffered so that they could enjoy a life full of possibilities.

-MIGUEL ALBA
Málaga City, Málaga, Andalucía, Spain
Spanish investigative writer and historian
Author: *S.S. Heliopolis, The First Emigration of Andalusians to Hawaii. 1907*

To live history through the memory of a beloved ancestor touches one's soul. Susan's focus on her grandfather's words reminds us of sacrifice, hardships, steadfastness and defines our humble beginnings as Spanish descendants.

- PATRICIA RUIZ STEELE
Author: *The Girl Immigrant*

Congratulations on doing such a wonderful job transforming these memories and sharing them with us all. Very few of our ancestors could put down in writing their experiences leaving Spain for Hawaii and then to the United States. Their memories bring a special meaning to us all. Of ....three recorded memories; by Joseph Lopez Lopez, Joseph Caamano Chang, and Cayetano Garcia Ciurana; Joseph Lopez's will be the first published. Best wishes from all of us at Hawaiian Spaniards.

- MIKE MUNOZ
"Hawaiian Spaniards" Facebook page Administrator
Compiler of a future publication of Hawaiian Spaniard stories.

Memoirs
Joseph L. Lopez

Joseph Lopez Lopez (José)

The Memoirs
of a Spanish Immigrant
to the United States

Edited, compiled and published by
Susan Marie (Hassinger Lopez) Burkholder
(Granddaughter of Joseph Lopez Lopez)

Memoirs
Joseph L. Lopez
Joseph Lopez Lopez
The Memoirs of a Spanish Immigrant to the United States

© 2020 Susan Burkholder: Editor, Compiler, Publisher

Printed in the United States of America
Prepared for publication by: Darlene Swanson • www.van-garde.com

Copyright 2020 by Susan Marie (Hassinger Lopez) Burkholder

ISBN: (Print Edition): 978-0-578-66033-2
ISBN: (eBook Edition): 978-0-578-68391-1
Library of Congress Control Number: 2020911133

Front Cover: Elizabeth Castle with E. Castle Art

Susan Burkholder can be reached at JoseLopezMemoirs@gmail.com

Contents

Acknowledgements

by Susan Marie (Hassinger Lopez) Burkholder

Thank you to:

TJ, my soul mate: Were ever two people more matched by God? Perhaps equally, but certainly not more than the two of us. You patiently understood as I spent hours working on this project. You matched my enthusiasm in finding Izbor and its winding steep paths. You embraced the adventure of discovering the history of Madrid and Andalucía, perhaps even more than I did. Far beyond those temporary pursuits, we have walked together through life. I am forever thankful that you have loved me…just as I am.

My mom, Jo (Josephine Lopez Hassinger): I so regret not making the time to take you to Spain. I miss you. You were one of my very best friends.

My dad, Neal (Russell Neal Hassinger): Spain was probably never on your radar. Yet you loved a Spanish woman and Jerry and I with the best you had to offer.

My brother, Jerry: Thank you for delving into technical book publishing issues. We see life from a different perspective, yet we share a history of being Hassinger Lopez. I wish you could have seen Andalucía with me. Thank you for being my big brother. I love you.

My niece, Megan; I pray you appreciate, embrace, assimilate your Spanish heritage. I love you beautiful girl.

The friends and relatives who encouraged me to persevere with publishing the writings of Joseph Lopez Lopez. You are many.

Notably:

> Jennifer Click, who sat with me for hours going line by line to ensure my grandfather's words were exactly represented; and who persisted in praying for this project and holding me accountable for making progress.

Karen Rader, who shared with me the concept of completion vs. perfection.

Hawaiian Spaniards Facebook: Administrators and Followers

Your enjoyment and appreciation of the altered ancestry version of my grandfather's writing prompted me to realize that others may want to read his *actual* words.

https://www.facebook.com/HawaiianSpaniard/

> Patricia Ruiz Steele (Author: *The Girl Immigrant*) and Gloria Lopez (Author*: An American Paella*) for helping me work through how to edit and publish.

> Patricia Ruiz Steele for Beta Reading the manuscript.

> Steve Alonzo for helping me know the history of the uploading and posting of the memoirs; connecting me to Miguel Alba

in Spain; doing research and sending me information from the ship manifests. Most fun of all, helping me know of the connection between his family and mine related to the use of a hillside in Hawaii. I enjoyed learning that we are cousins by marriage. Your mother's first cousin, Sally Escano; married my grandmother's first cousin, James Perez.

Jim Fernandez for helping me know where to find Izbor, Spain; encouraging me to publish the memoirs; and for creating <u>Invisible Immigrants</u> with Luis Arego. The photo in your book of the Escano market in Vacaville prompted Steve Alonzo and I to discover the connection between his family and mine.

Mike Munoz for posting the altered version on Hawaiian Spaniards which sparked interest among others whose forefathers made the journey; for communicating with me at length about the memoirs; and for helping me work through the decision to publish the memoirs as a standalone book

Nicole Henares for prompting me to think in a broader perspective about immigrants both past and present; for communicating with me about the strength of our female forbearers; and for being a shining example herself of what it means to be a strong, independent descendant of Spanish women. Thank you for listening to my perspective, as I have listened to yours.

The additional administrators for the Hawaiian Spaniards page not mentioned above: Larry Campos and Joey Vilchez Nardone.

Miguel Alba, Spanish historian and author on the topic of the Spanish movement to Hawaii... (*S.S. Heliopolis, The First Emigration of Andalusians to Hawaii. 1907)* for including excerpts from my grandfather's memoirs in your Spanish books related to the emigration of Spaniards to Hawaii.

Dan Stoe for publishing the altered version of the memoirs on Ancestry.com. In addition to making Joseph Lopez Lopez's writings known; thank you for noting in your ancestry posting that the version had been altered and that additional information had been added to it. Dan, please connect with me via JoseLopezMemoirs@ gmail.com. I think I have determined that you are connected via my grandfather's sister, Delores/Laura

Lisa Anderson, (granddaughter of my mother's cousin Presentacíon Maria Ruiz/PR), who sent my mother a partial family tree in 2004. The information you sent to my mother has been instrumental in piecing together our shared ancestry.

My brother-in-Christ, Luis Arizpe, for translating my grandmother's birth documents. You made it possible for us to find her birthplace and connect to her heritage in Montellano.

Antonio Gil. Our primary guide in Andalucía. You went above and beyond in helping us find Izbor and our family there. You befriended and drew out people as we trekked up through the village; eventually finding my distant cousin. You went above and beyond in trying to do the same in Montellano. But beyond all of that, you became our friend. We learned Spanish history and culture from you; and we laughed together over movie references together (Jack Lemmon and Walter Matthau...which was TJ? which was you?)

Gary Montague, Owner of Tour Andalucía International in Mollina, Málaga, Spain; and the staff at Tour Andalucía: In addition to Antonio: Barry, Rob, Alex, Jimmy; and of course, Liz, who made us breakfast each morning. You all created a home base from which we could explore Andalucía and were our guides in learning Andalucía.

Our companions in Andalucía: the Canadians: Debbie, Gordon, Ruth, Gerry, Peggy and Paul; the British: Mary, Mel, Christine and Alan; the Australians: Ann and Tony; the Floridians; Will, Julie, Pam and Kevin. Thank you for conversations during van rides, over churros, honey/eggplant appetizers, wine, dinners and final paella night. We learned so much from seeing things from your side of the window. I hope you also learned a bit from seeing things from the Texas side of the same window.

And most importantly, thank you Grandpa. For putting pen to paper in 1978 and bequeathing your story to us.

   Con mucho amor, respeto, y admiración
Tu nieta;
Susan Marie (Hassinger Lopez) Burkholder

Preface

by Susan Marie (Hassinger Lopez) Burkholder

JOSEPH LOPEZ LOPEZ'S (JOSÉ) WROTE his memoirs by hand on lined notebook paper in 1978. These pages were "bound" into a gray folder. Copies were given to his children and his grandchildren. Copies were also distributed to other relatives. I have the copy that was given to my mother, Josephine. My cousin, Gary Gass, has the original hand written copy given to his mother, Mary.

1966 I was 4. You were 66.

These memoirs encompasses Joseph Lopez Lopez's recollections of his life; from the early 1900's, through the time of his putting pen to paper in 1978.

Joseph Lopez Lopez's parents moved their family to Hawaii from the Andalucía region of Spain in 1907. From 1907 to 1913, six ships brought approximately 8000 men, women and children from Spain to the sugar cane fields of Hawaii. Most of these Spaniards subsequently immigrated to California.

The primary goal in publishing Joseph Lopez Lopez's memoirs is to allow his descendants, and the descendants of other Hawaiian Spaniards to have this history.

"In the early 1990s, memoirs written by ordinary people experienced a sudden upsurge, as an increasing number of people realized that their ancestors' *and their own stories were about to disappear... At the same time...research began to show that familiarity with* genealogy *helps people find their place in the world and that life review helps people come to terms with their own past."*

—Wikipedia: https://en.wikipedia.org/wiki/Memoir

"Memoirs written as a way to pass down a personal legacy, rather than as a literary work of art or historical document, are emerging as a personal and family responsibility."

—Wikipedia: https://en.wikipedia.org/wiki/Memoir
Balzer, Paula (2011). *Writing & Selling Your Memoir: How to Craft Your Life Story So That Somebody Else Will Actually Want to Read It.* ISBN 978-1599631356.

Secondarily, publishing Joseph Lopez Lopez's memoirs allows others a glimpse into the life of a Spanish immigrant family, from 1900 through 1978; as they courageously leave their impoverished ancestral home in the Andalucía region of Spain, travel to Hawaii, and eventually immigrate permanently to California.

As a child and young adult, I viewed my grandfather's story from *my* perspective...that of a well-assimilated granddaughter of a Spanish immigrant.

As I read and re-read my grandfather's writings over the past few years in working on this project, I was able to better see *his* perspective. I came to understand the nuances of what it meant to immigrate, to assimilate to a new life. My perspective changed as I came around and looked through his eyes; saw what he saw from his perspective.

If you and I are looking through the same window, but from opposite sides, our views of what we are seeing through that exact same window will always be different. You see the outdoors looking out your kitchen window. I, looking through that same window from the outdoors, see a kitchen. We are both correct...just a different perspective. It is only when we take the time to come around to the other side of the window that we can "see" another's perspective. I pray that those reading my grandfather's memoirs "see" a new perspective.

"...we don't have to become a 'melting pot' where we lose our identities...we can be the 'tossed salad' where we maintain our own distinct flavors and at the same time become an integral part of the whole America..."
  —From a social media post. No author was credited.

This melting pot vs. tossed salad concept exemplifies a wider perspective of the varied immigrant heritage of the United States.

Let us each be encouraged to delve into the story of our own family's immigration story. It is perhaps not as clear as we thought it was.

We are all from somewhere else; ...no matter how far back that may be.

—Susan Marie (Hassinger Lopez) Burkholder

Edits

IN MY EDITING, I TRIED to preserve the original vernacular, intent and meaning behind what my grandfather wrote.

Joseph Lopez Lopez left Spain when he was seven, lived in Hawaii until he was twelve, and did not complete formal education in California beyond the sixth grade. I have always appreciated my grandfather's self-taught English and his ability to articulate his thoughts in written and spoken word in both Spanish and English.

As a high school student, I took Spanish for two years. I wrote to my grandfather in "Spanish". My grandfather wrote back in the Spanish he knew, and included my original letter lovingly corrected in red pen as to "proper" Spanish. I wrote in the Spanish learned in a public school in Texas. He wrote back in the Spanish of a Spaniard.

Therefore, I chose **not** to significantly alter my grandfather's writing. For ease of reading and understanding; I have made *mild* edits to grammatical issues such as punctuation, verb tense and pronoun use. Edits are limited as much as possible to preserve my grandfather's Spanish vernacular and sentence structure; allowing his story to unfold exactly as he wrote it. I realize that his writing is not polished; yet, I am choosing **not** to significantly correct it.

A few details of personal family situations are tastefully edited as well.

My grandfather did not break up his narrative with chapters or breaks. For ease of reading and understanding, I chose to separate long sections into paragraphs and to add **headings** to sections. These headings are designated in **Bold Text** and were ***not*** part of the original writings of my grandfather.

Where necessary, I have added side notes to clarify or provide context. These notes are designated in **text boxes.**

Photos and documents were added to complement my grandfather's writings.

Original Version vs.
Altered Versions

An altered version of my grandfather's memoirs was created at some point by an unknown person. Changes in wording, order and content; as well as additions and deletions of words and concepts resulted in a version which is different in many ways from the original writing of Joseph Lopez Lopez.

This altered version was uploaded to ancestry.com and subsequently to Facebook.

I am thankful to those who uploaded and posted the altered version, because those postings connected me to the Hawaiian Spaniards Facebook page; from which I have benefitted greatly.

In general, the alterations were harmless; however in a few incidences, the alterations completely changed the actual content, meaning, and intent of what my grandfather originally wrote.

One Example:
Joseph Lopez Lopez wrote of passing through the Golden Gate in 1912, when his family arrived in the San Francisco Bay from Hawaii.

way. On July 17-1912 at day brake we were going through the golden gate it was dark, all we could see were a few lights

The transcribed version uploaded to ancestry.com; and later to Facebook:

"On July 17, 1912, at daybreak, we were going under the Golden Gate Bridge. It was dark and all we could see was a few lights."

Do you see the difference? The **_addition_** of the words "**under**" and "**Bridge**"? The change of verb tense from "**were**" to "**was**"?

Given that the "**_Bridge_**" did not exist in 1912, there were *negative* Facebook comments questioning the **veracity** of my grandfather's memoirs. Subsequent kind comments tried to "excuse" his writing as that of an "an old man" recalling events from a long time ago.

When in reality, Joseph Lopez Lopez knew **_exactly_** what he was writing about **at 78 years old,** when he recalled this memory **from 66 years before, when he was 12.** The statement, "going through the golden gate" **_is_** correct. The Golden Gate is the name given by John C. Fremont in 1846 to the **strait** into the San Francisco Bay; *long* before a bridge was built with the same name. My grandfather knew this. The person who chose to alter his writings did not. My grandfather's verb tense of were vs. was: Correct as well. All **we** could see **was…**(incorrect use of verb tense) vs. what my grandfather wrote: All **we** could see **were..** (correct us of verb tense).

Appendices

The information on Cuba and Olives were added by José to his memoirs.

Cuba:
José's writings about Cuba reveal how he viewed the Cuba conflict through his window; based primarily upon what he heard, as verbally told, from his own father's personal experience and perspective.

Olives:
Joseph Lopez Lopez's recipe for Spanish Olives.

Appendices added by Susan Burkholder:

Family Photos

Family Trees:
Joseph Lopez Lopez
    Forbearers and Siblings
    Descendants
    Aunts, Uncles, Cousins

Josefa (Josie/Josephine) Borrego Romero
    Forbearers
    Aunts and Uncles
    Siblings and their descendants

Ship Manifests for Montellano born Families (Borrego, Romero, Terez)

Josefa BORREGO Perez's Birth, Baptism Documents

Translation of Birth, Baptism Documents by Luis Arizpe

Location of the Lopez and Borrego Families in Hawaii

Alphabetical Family and Friend List:
So readers might easily find their relatives amongst José's stories.

MEMOIRS

JOSEPH L. LOPEZ

Cover of Joseph Lopez Lopez's Original Memoirs

on request of my children and grandchildren
I am writing my memoirs or roots.
This is not fiction, but facts as I remember them
I am at present of sound mind.
I Joseph Lopez Lopez (Jose) was born on april 10
1900, in a little village by the name Isbor del
Rio. provincia (province) of Granada, Spain
about 80 Kilometers south of Granada and 18
Kilometers north of the mediteraen sea
My father name was manuel Lopez Bilbao
was born on February 1876 and died August 1945
of cancer of the throat in O'conner Hospital
in San Jose California.
My mother name was maria Lopez Diaz.
she was born march 1877 and died July 1957
in the Hospital in auborn California after
surgery for cancer of the liver, she was over
80 years old.
My grandfather on my father side, name
was Jose Ramon Lopez was born 1850 and
died in 1898. While my father was in the
Spanish American war in cuba, he was a
redhead man. he fell from a cliff while
earing for some sheep and goats
he was a sherperd. some body said he
was pushed over the cliff.

Page 1 of Joseph Lopez Lopez's handwritten memoirs

2

Memoirs

Joseph L. Lopez

Bold section headings added by Susan Burkholder.

Family Lineage

On request of my children and grandchildren, I am writing my memoirs or roots. This is not fiction, but facts as I remember them. I am, at present, of sound mind.

I, Joseph Lopez Lopez (José), was born on April 10, 1900, in a little village by the name of Izbor del Rio; provincia (province) of Granada, Spain; about 80 kilometers south of Granada and 18 kilometers north of the Mediterranean Sea.

[Susan Burkholder 2017. Izbor]

Starting point: IZBOR: A little more than ½ way between Granada and Motril. First **Day's Journey:** IZBOR to ALMUÑECAR 42 km / 26 miles. ALMUÑECAR is on the coast about ½ way between Motril and NERJA. **Second Day:** ALMUÑECAR to NERJA 22 km/ 14 miles. **Final Day of Walking:** NERJA to MÁLAGA is 55 km/34 miles.

My father's name was Manuel Lopez Bilbao. He was born in February, 1876 and died in August, 1945 of cancer of the throat in O'Connor Hospital in San Jose, California.

My mother's name was Maria Lopez Diaz. She was born in March, 1877 and died in July, 1957 in the hospital in Auburn, California after surgery for cancer of the liver. She was over 80 years old.

My grandfather on my father's side was named José Ramon

Lopez. He was born in 1850 and died in 1898, while my father was in the Spanish-American War in Cuba. My grandfather was a redheaded man. He fell from a cliff while caring for some sheep and goats. He was a shepherd. Somebody said he was pushed over the cliff. When my father returned from Cuba, he tried to find out who did it; but nobody said anything. Up to today, nobody seems to know the truth.

My grandmother on my father's side was named Maria Bilbao Alvarez. She was born in 1852 and died in 1903 of cancer of the uterus. She was a tall, dark complexed woman.

My grandfather on my mother's side was named Antonio Lopez Lopez. He was born in 1852 and died in 1918 in that great Spanish influencia (flu). He was a farmer. He had some olive trees, some almond trees and some vegetable patches. In that part of the country, the land is rough and steep. Many years ago, people built stone walls eight and ten feet high, then cut the dirt and filled the space with it. The hill side looks like steps. They planted their vegetables on the flat spaces. They had plenty of water from the Sierra Nevada Mountains.

My grandmother on my mother's side was named Maria de Cruz Diaz Lopez. She was born in 1854 and died in 1936 of old age.

In the Spanish speaking world, a woman does not lose her maiden name when she marries; thereby, when a child is born they give its first name, then the father's second name and the mother's second name is the third name of the child.

Spain: Early Years and Departure to Hawaii

When I was three years old I fell from an almond tree at Grandpa's place and landed on my head, and cut my scalp real bad. They could not stop the bleeding and there was no doctor in the village. They patched me up the best way they could and hair grew over it. Today the hair is gone and the scar shows.

(Susan Burkholder 2017. Izbor]

I also remember there is a bridge and a tunnel by the village built by Moors centuries ago. When Queen Isabella drove the Moors from Granada in 1490 they used this bridge to go to the Mediterranean Sea and across into Morocco. Today it is a highway.

In 1906 they were advertising free immigration to Brazil, South America and my father was one of the first to enlist for Brazil. But later he learned there was an insect called nigua that developed in your toe nails. He had it in Cuba. He suffered very much with it in Cuba while he was in the service during the Spanish-American War.

Six months later there was another advertisement for immigration to Hawaii, offering 24 dollars gold each month to work in the sugar cane fields. The deal was they give each family one acre of land with a house on it; free doctor and hospital for the whole family; and school education for the children; if the families would stay 3 years. After 3 years, the land and house was yours. So my father took that chance with seven other families from the same village.

In January 1907, very early in the morning, they got me up from bed. I was sleeping with my Grandpa Lopez. I was not 7 years yet. My Uncle Patricio, my father's brother, carried me on his back to the *parador*, an inn alongside the main road. We waited for a two wheel wagon and a mule pulling it.

The whole family was there crying and saying never to see each other again. My Uncle Patricio was my father's brother. He was a tall, very fair, handsome man. In a few days, he was leaving for the Spanish Army in Morocco and Spanish West Africa. After he served 3 years, he was discharged from the army. He never went to Spain again. He went to Ceuta, a Spanish sea port and fortification across the Strait of Gibraltar and married a girl from the same village he came from. Her father was sent to life in prison there [Cueta] for a crime he committed in Spain.

After saying goodbye and a lot of crying, we left the *parador* on the wagon and started for the sea port of Málaga. It took us 3 days to get there, only 90 kilometers. We could walk faster than the wagon could move. The first night we stopped in a town named Almuñecar by the Mediterranean Sea. The second day we stopped at a little town close to Málaga, by the name of Nerja. The third day we reached Málaga.

EMIGRACION CON PASAJE GRATUITO AL ESTADO
DE HAWAI,
(ESTADOS-UNIDOS DE AMÉRICA)
Descripción de las Islas Haway, según el célebre viajero M. C. de Variony

......Es punto menos que imposible hacer comprender, á quien no los ha disfrutado, los incomparables atractivos del clima de las Islas de Hawai. Una temperatura constantemente igual, que todo lo mas varia diez grados, y que casi siempre está á 30° centígrados; un cielo purísimo, apenas velado de vez en cuando por frescas nubecillas y lluvias oportunas; una naturaleza alegre y lozana, admirablemente iluminada por un sol radiante, constituyen el atractivo mas poderoso para atraer al extranjero y obligarle á prolongar su permanencia en aquellas Islas. Las tempestades son muy raras allí, tan raras como los huracanes, que suelen ser el azote de los países intertropicales; las noches, sobre todo, son sumamente apacibles, y cuando brilla la luna, envolviendo las campiñas en los suaves y misteriosos efluvios de sus rayos, cualquiera se creería víctima de una ilusión encantadora. Es tan pura y despejada la atmósfera que á media noche se puede leer á la claridad combinada de la luz y las estrellas. En ninguna parte se extiende la vía láctea con tanto explendor y majestad como allí: las constelaciones invisibles en Europa, iluminan el espacio y brillan como deslumbradoras perlas; el mar despliega en la costa sus oleadas fosforescentes y mece sus plácidos ensueños con lento y monótono movimiento......

Los emigrantes Españoles que quieran acoerse á las concesiones y beneficios que ofrecen as Leyes de Inmigración y Colonización del Estado de HAWAI, obtienen pasage gratuito desde Málaga para dicho Estado, en magníficos Vapores de marcha rápida, de más le 12.000 toneladas, con comida, durante el viaje, á la Española, condimentada por cocineros embarcados expresamente para ello.

El Gobierno de dicho Estado, bajo cuya gaatía se efectúa la emigración, ofrece, á los SEMBRADORES AGRICULTORES un porvenir halagüeño, cuyas ventajas son las siguientes:

Los varones cabeza de familia

20 duros americanos oro, al mes, durante el primer año de trabajo.

21 duros americanos oro, al mes, durante el segundo año.

22 duros americanos oro, al mes, durante el tercer año.

bus mujeres, sus esposas 12 duros oro al mes.

bus demás individuos de su familia que sean mayores de 15 años, 15 duros mensuales, si son varones y 10 duros si son hembras.

Desde que desembarquen, se les facilita una magnífica casa-vivienda (que vale más de 300 pesos oro) agua y lumbre y escuela gratuita, donde reciben educación los hijos menores, para los que es obligatorio asistir á ella.

Y á los tres años de trabajo, con buena conducta y en los que hayan demostrado que son buenos Labradores (y especialmente para el cultivo de la caña de azúcar), se les cede gratuitamente y en propiedad absoluta y sin gravámen alguno, la casa donde estén viviendo y además una fanega de tierra.

Condiciones que deben reunir los emigrantes

Es condición indispensable que los emigrantes sean **agricultores** que gozen de buena salud, no padezcan de la vista, que no tengan defectos físicos y se formen precisamente **familias** cuya constitución puede ser, como sigue:

1.° Marido y mujer sin hijos, no teniendo el marido **más de 45 años**, ni la mujer **más de 40.**

2.° Marido y mujer con hijos, no pudiendo los jefes tener más de 45 años, con tal que haya en la familia un hombre útil **de 17 á 45 años.**

3.° Viudo ó viuda, teniendo siempre un hombre útil **mayor de 17 años y menor de 45 años.**

4.° Hombre casado no llevando la mujer, pero sí llevando hijos con tal que haya siempre un hombre útil de 17 á 45 años.

5.° Mujer casada no llevando su marido, pero sí llevando hijos con tal que haya uno útil de **17 á 45 años.**

Podrán ir como agregados á las familias antes expresadas, todos los parientes, carnales y políticos, menores de 40 años. Las personas mayores de 45 años que no gozan de pasaje gratuito, estas tienen que pagarse el pasage cuesta Pesetas 400.

Documentos que necesitan presentar las familias que deseen emigrar

1.° Cédula personal para todos los mayores de 14 años.

2.° Los varones y mujeres solteras, hasta la edad de 23 años, una autorización de sus padres ó tutores, otorgada ante Notario ó ante el Alcalde del pueblo de su vecindad. Este documento no es necesario cuando vayan en compañía de sus padres, pero en todo caso las mujeres solteras han de presentar un certificado que acredite su estado de soltería.

3.° Partida de bautismo para todos los varones y mujeres solteras.

4.° Los varones de 15 á 20 años no pueden embarcar sin presentar un certificado que acredite haber consignado en la Caja de Depósito la suma de 500 pesetas á las resultas de la quinta, según previene la ley.

5.° Los varones de 20 á 40 años han de presentar la licencia absoluta si son licenciados definitivos. Los que pertenezcan á la reserva ó á la clase de reclutas disponibles han de presentar un permiso del Capitán General del distrito respectivo, autorizándoles para efectuar su embarque ó ausentarse de la Península. Este documento no puede tener más de 4 meses á contarse desde la fecha de su expedición.

6.° Las mujeres casadas que no vayan acompañadas de sus maridos han de presentar un permiso de éste, visado por la Alcaldía del pueblo de su vecindad ó por Notario, siendo en la Capital.

7.° Partida de casamiento para los matrimonios.

8.° Partida de viudedad para las viudas.

9.° Certificado de buena conducta expedido por la Alcaldía de su residencia con las senas personales, para todos los individuos mayores de 14 años.

10 Certificado de no estar procesado, expedido por el Juzgado del pueblo donde residan, para todos los mayores de 14 años, ó de la Audiencia siendo en la Capital.

DESCONFIAR DE LOS INTERMEDIARIOS
Para mayores detalles y presentación de documentos:
DON CARLOS CROVETTO, Encargado del Departamento de Revisión
CALLE DE RIOS ROSAS (antes Cañón) núm. 3.--Málaga

7

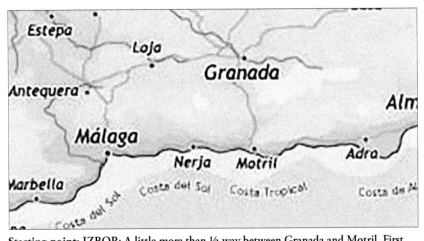

Starting point: IZBOR: A little more than ½ way between Granada and Motril. First Day's Journey: IZBOR to ALMUÑECAR 42 km / 26 miles. ALMUÑECAR is on the coast about ½ way between Motril and NERJA.
Second Day: ALMUÑECAR to NERJA 22 km/ 14 miles.
Final Day of Walking: NERJA to MÁLAGA is 55 km/34 miles.

There we lived in a *posada* (inn) and waited for the ship to come. My folks bought a new trunk with a round top which they kept until we lived in Chico, California. They also bought two blankets that lasted many years.

While we were waiting for the ship, my parents almost ran out of money, so they fed us until the ship came. I do not know if the government fed us or the sugar cane companies from Hawaii did. Finally the steamer arrived and anchored 6 kilometers (3 miles) out from port. My father spent the last two *pesetas* (40¢) for a rowboat to take us to the ship.

A few days before we got on the ship, my father gave us a boat ride by the Alameda Park by the sea and there were cement steps by the water's edge. I never forgot these steps. In 1949, when I went to Spain, we went to Málaga and there they were – nothing changed. [Susan Burkholder 2017. Cement Steps Malaga]

Finally we reached the ship - it was night time. We got to the large barge alongside the ship. I remember there were a lot of armed policemen on deck. They were keeping military age men from getting aboard. This happened on the 7th of March, 1907. On the first day, the Chinese cooks burned the first meal which was rice. Half of the people that lived in Málaga got off the ship. We could not. My father would never go back to that misery again. So we stayed on board the S.S. Leopoli. I heard after that was not the real name. It was an English ship named after a Greek island. It had no cabins on deck except the captain's quarters. All the people stayed below deck in large compartments full with double deck tiny beds, packed together. Just imagine no baths, no showers, only pots. Half of the people got sea sick.

The Spanish people pronounced the name of the ship I came in Leopoli. But the English people pronounce it different. The only person that knows the right pronunciation is Marina Lippertz, who lives in Mountain View.

S.S. Heliopolis sailed from Málaga, Spain in 1907
https://en.wikipedia.org/wiki/Spanish_immigration_to_Hawaii
(Note: There is another ship by the same name.)

The men went on deck for their bowel movements. There was a long trough that looked like a bath tub with swift running water. I was afraid to use it; the water might flush me away. Some people had lice, in a few days everybody was infested, even the captain.

The ship had an all Chinese crew. A few days out at sea, they fed us macaroni and sea biscuits, hard as bricks. There was plenty of good food aboard, but they did not cook it for us. Kids used to steal potatoes from the cellar and cook them on steam pipes that came from the engine room; so their mothers could make potato salad with olive oil which they had aboard. The men had to steal the oil.

I remember the kids used to unsew the life savers and get the cork out to make toys. Just imagine if the ship would have sunk. All the beds had life savers as mattresses.

A few days after we left Málaga it got very hot and they put some canvas over and above our heads to keep the heat out. We were crossing the equator.

A few days after that we had an accident. A few boys were playing on deck and the crew of the ship was working and left the hatch door open and one boy fell to the bottom of the cellar and got killed.

There was also some dancing and singing aboard ship in the evenings.

About 25 days out at sea, we stopped at a seaport named Punta Arenas in Chile,

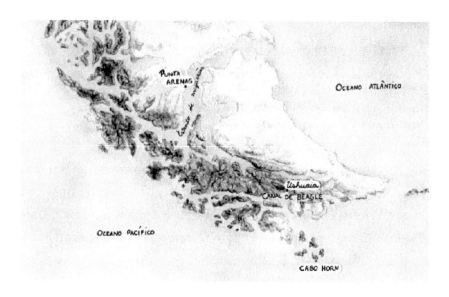

Just before entering the Strait of Magellan, we got fresh water and supplies, and the crew went in the cellar of the ship and brought out a lot of cod fish. It was rotten and full of worms. They starved us with macaroni and sea biscuits and the good food went to waste. The ship was a little way from port, some people came with row boats alongside the ship and they spoke Spanish and told us to come over to Chile. They had plenty of work and a lot of land.

They told us the place we were going the people spoke like dogs barking. A lot of people got off the ship. My father was ready to get on the rope ladder and leave everything behind, but my mother did not have the nerve to get down the ladder to the waiting boats. If we had stayed in Chile, we would have been wealthy people today. Those that did stay wrote to us and said they were great land owners.

So, we stayed with the ship. A few days after that, we went through the Strait of Magellan. Just before we came out of the Strait, the captain ordered everybody below deck and shut all hatch doors. It was very cold and the Pacific Ocean was very, very rough. Just imagine how rough it gets. This same ship, on its return trip, went to the bottom in the same spot. It is known over the world as the graveyard of ships for many centuries. We made it alright.

After a few days in the Pacific Ocean, Marina Lippertz was born. Her parents were going to name her Pacifica, finally, they didn't like the name and called her Marina.

After a few more days, it got very hot again. We were crossing the equator again. One week before we reached Honolulu, Bert Ojeda was born. My sister, Rose, was born on the big island of Hawaii a few months after.

Hawaii
1907-1912

The ship arrived in Honolulu, Hawaii on April 26, 1907 at night. The passengers got off on April 28, 1907. They put us in a big immigration building. They fed us good food. Nobody was sick. They kept us three days there. In the meantime, the big 5 sugar cane companies kept the families they needed in each island. We went to the big island, and all the people from the same village, Izbor del Rio, did too.

I remember getting on a small ship or a boat. We all stayed on deck – the only place we could ride. We spent the night on deck and arrived in Hilo, Hawaii the next day just about sundown. Hilo had no harbor, so they got us out on rowboats to some wagons waiting for us to our destination plantation: Hamaulo, Camp 4; three miles up hill. It was pouring down rain, like it usually does on that island. After we got settled on our wagons, we started for our camp. First we came to Camp 1.

It was a Portuguese camp. Then Camp 2, it was Filipino camp. Then Camp 3, it was Japanese Camp. Our camp was the last one high up on the mountains. The higher we went, the more it rained.

A baby was crying as we went by Camp 3. Some woman made a silly remark that the cry sounded like a baby crying, not like dogs barking as they told us. Finally we reached Camp 4. There was a one-room school house. The men went in and each got a number. There were thirty families and only ten houses.

They put all the numbers in a box and shook it. Each family picked a number, three families to a house. My father picked one close to the school house with two other families. Every acre of land had a house. All in rows about fifty feet apart. We couldn't see them with the jungle and nighttime. Also, a wagon followed us with some groceries. My first meal on the big island was corn beef and soda crackers.

Before I forget, we were the first Spanish immigrants in Hawaii to work in the sugar cane fields.

The Hawaiian Islands used to belong to England. They used to call them the Sandwich Islands. Later it was discovered that sugar cane could be grown there. Believe me, the best in the world – with all that rain and volcanic soil.

The next few days they brought some Japanese carpenters and built more houses. One for each family. They were built with 1 x 12 boards, straight up and down; had two bedrooms, one living room and dining room. The kitchen was connected by a corridor with galvanized roofs and a little outhouse fifty feet away.

Finally each family had a house. My father drew number 7 on the main street. There my sister, Antonia (Rose) was born on August 4, 1907; the first baby to be born in camp. My father didn't like the house and acre of land. It had a spring in the middle and everybody came there to wash clothes and for drinking water. Later a family moved away from number 10 and we moved into it. You could not see it thirty feet away with the jungle around the house. My father worked 6 days a week. On Sundays and evenings, he began to clear the land of giant ferns and orchids tangled together with some passion fruit vines. We tried to burn the damn stuff, but it wouldn't burn, so we piled it. It never dried, so it rotted in piles.

I was about eight years old then. I cut brush and piled it up with my father. Then it was all clear. My father hired a man with a team of horses and plowed the ground, and we planted sugar cane. After it came up, we had to hoe weeds away from the canes, it rained so much. The weeds grew very fast. We couldn't get rid of the weeds. Here in California, we have these weeds in flower pots, well protected from frost. It took 18 months to grow the first crop of sugar cane. It brought in 150 dollars. That was a fortune.

My father hired some Japanese and some friends to cut the sugar cane in one Sunday, and pile it along the flume the plantation built. The flume went through all the neighbors' land. The flume was half full of water, which carried the canes, about four feet long, to the mill by the ocean. All the land on that island slopes toward the ocean, with three active volcanoes in the middle of the island.

The men folks had to go and work for the sugar cane company. That was the contract they signed in Spain before we came. It was for three years. That way the land and house was ours.

Some of the people said afterwards that we were in bondage and came in a cattle ship. The women and kids over nine years of age went to work too. Women earned 45¢ a day for ten hours. Kids earned 25¢ a day for the same hours. When boys reached 14 years, they went to work with the men, getting the same pay. I started to earn 25 ¢ a day when I was nine years of age.

I started school when I was eight years of age in the one-room schoolhouse. Big kids and small, all in one room. Nobody knew a word of English. There I learned my A, B, Cs and the rest of it, until I reached twelve years. I was in the third grade when we left the Hawaiian Islands.

I also remember one morning we were pledging allegiance to the flag of the United States of America. The flag was in direct line with the Kilauea volcano. A big cloud of smoke came out of the volcano and the earth began to shake. The earthquakes were quite often.

Also, there in the same camp by the schoolhouse lived Emily Calvo and her folks. Her name was Emilia Lozano then. By her lived her uncle, named Espigares, Joe Espigares. Emily's cousin is now the Yolo County supervisor.

We went bare foot, never bought a pair of shoes until we came to California. The kids had athlete's foot. It was very painful when dirt got between our toes.

When I was about 10 years old, on school vacation, all the working kids were walking to work. Tony Escano's big brothers and my big cousin decided to have some fun with us, so they started a fight with me and Tony Escano. I didn't want to, neither did Tony Escano. So they coached us so much, we said alright, we will fight. I got ready and they switched Tony and put his big brother, Edward Escano, in his place. I was not afraid of Tony, but Edward Escano was too big for me. I was afraid of him. He came and knocked me down and had me down. I couldn't move. So with one hand, I got hold of his arm and sunk my eye teeth in his arm. That stopped the fight and we became good friends after that.

I worked in the sugar cane fields until July 1, 1912.

During the years we stayed in Hamaulo Camp 4, my father had some horses. When I was ten years of age, he bought me one. I didn't have a saddle, so he put an old blanket and cinched it to the horse. I had to ride the horse that way. One Sunday, he and I went to a different camp to get some sweet potatoes and his horse went full gallop and my horse followed with me hanging on for dear life. But I didn't fall that time. The following year, I was sent to get his pay on payday on my horse. I couldn't get on it, so I led him by a rock or tree stump that way I got on. As I approached the pay station, the horse got scared and stopped suddenly and I went over his head. I didn't get hurt.

On the big island of Hawaii there are three volcanoes and the land slopes toward the ocean. There are also deep canyons. The land cannot be cultivated. My father asked permission to clear the land. It was very steep, so he cleared two places and planted sugar cane on it. It looked like steps of a house, rows of cane above one another. We harvested one crop. Later when we left for California, my dad sold it to Mr. Escano, Sr., also the horses.

While we lived on the plantation the older folks built ovens to bake bread. Some people call them Dutch ovens. My mother baked very good bread, even the Russians used them. I forgot to say there were Russian immigrants that came to live in Camp 4, but they didn't stay long.

Also in 1910, the Japanese kids stopped coming to our school in Camp 4. We didn't know what was the trouble. Later, they told us that President Taft stopped the education for all Asiatics. A few days later three Japanese war ships appeared in Hilo Bay. At night they had searchlights all over the cane fields. I didn't know what they were. My father told what it was. A month later the Japanese kids returned to school.

In the spring of 1911, another Spanish immigration came. This time through Gibraltar. Another in the spring, also another in the fall. The last one in 1913, all through Gibraltar. They built many more houses for them. They had it real easy compared with us. We were the first of the people that came with us from the village. Six families remained with us in Camp 4. One family was turned back from Málaga. The lady had red eyes. Everybody had to be in perfect health.

When I was going to school in the plantation, I was 11 years old in the second grade. My cousin, Tony Lopez, another boy, and myself decided to go to Catholic school in Hilo, Hawaii. We had to walk 3 miles each way. We thought we were not learning enough in the public school.

So all three of us started school in Hilo. After a month of school, one morning, we decided to play marbles as we walked to school. Raining as it was, we threw the marbles along the road as we walked. That day, we got there late for class. The men teachers were waiting for us. They had bamboo switches. One by one, they hit our legs with the bamboo thin switches. We had short pants to our knees. They really cut our legs very bad. That was the end of my Catholic education.

We didn't like it anyway. Nothing but men teachers. We had to pray as we went to class and pray again as we came out, so we went back to our regular school.

After those first Spanish immigrations came to Hawaii, the big five companies stopped all Spanish immigration. They paid all expenses, and the Spanish people would not stay in the islands. 98% are here in California.

In all, six Spanish immigrant ships came to Hawaii. The last to arrive was in June of 1913.
https://en.wikipedia.org/wiki/Spanish_immigration_to_Hawaii

Ship Name	Port of Departure	Departure	Arrive Hawaii	Reference
Heliopolis	Malaga , Spain	Mar. 8, 1907	Apr. 26, 1907	Traces of Spain in the US
Orteric	Gibraltar, Gr. Britain	Feb. 24, 1911	Apr. 13, 1911	Your Island Routes
Willesden 1911	Gibraltar, Gr. Britain	Oct. 12, 1911	Dec. 3, 1911	Report of Federal Security Agency
Harpalion	Gibraltar, Gr. Britain	Feb. 22, 1912	Apr. 14, 1912	Your Island Routes
Willesden 1913	Gibraltar, Gr. Britain	Feb. 10, 1913	Mar 30, 1913	Your Island Routes
Ascot	Gibraltar, Gr. Britain	Apr. 12, 1913	Jun. 4, 1913	Your Island Routes

The "Big Five" controlled the sugar cane industry from the mid 1800's through the late 1900's.
https://en.wikipedia.org/wiki/Big_Five_(Hawaii)

Then they brought in one immigration after another; Japanese, Philippine and Chinese, which stayed and mixed with the Hawaiian people. That is why there is very little left of the Hawaiian race. Japanese are the majority race in Hawaii today.

One of the main reasons the Spanish people didn't stay in the islands was they were rather young people; between the ages of 25 and 35; and children 10 to 15 years old.

The Filipinos were coming around the Spanish girls and our parents did not want any mixture with Asians. 2% did mix. Even though we lived in different camps one mile apart, the Filipinos came to our camp and tried to give gifts to the girls, but the Spanish boys cut some sugar cane and made clubs with them, beat the hell out of the Filipinos. They never tried it again.

The working conditions were very bad. It rained nearly every day. Workers carried their lunch, and raincoat, and a hoe every working day. Also, they had to be at the schoolhouse yard at 6 A.M. From there, different gangs went to different fields. One morning while the men were walking to work, one big (luna), big boss on horseback, was rushing the men to a faster walk to work. But the men kept the same pace. He got angry and kicked one of the men in the back and hurt him badly. The other workers grabbed the horse and rider and threw them over a ravine. They never tried that again with the Spanish people.

One morning, before my father and mother went to work, he told me to do some work in the canes and to take care of my two sisters after school. That day my cousin Joe and I didn't go to school. About 2 P.M., that day, here comes the (hookie cop); some kind of school police; and a bunch of school boys, looking for us. We ran through the field. They also had a dog. My cousin Joe slipped away. Then they came after me. I couldn't get away then. So I jumped over a bank on some blackberry bushes 10 feet below; and I got away along a creek. My face was scratched and clothes all wet. I hid in the bushes until my folks came from work, and boy, did I get it. I never played hookie again.

Back of us lived Joe Santaella's folks. Joe lives now in Sunnyvale, California. He used to be head foreman in Libby's cannery.

Carmen Diaz and her folks came in the same ship, but lived in the next plantation. Also two large families that now live in Fairfield, California.

John Perez of Tracy, California and his folks came with us in the same ship, but didn't live in the same island.

The old folks, not so old than to have good times; they gathered in some friend's house who could play the guitar and bought some wine, and danced the fandango and had a great time. My father loved his wine and the fandango too. I used to go with him. He used to take a stick and wrap some burlap sack to one end of the stick and soak it in kerosene and light it. That lasted us until we reached the friend's house and later, back home. I used to fall asleep in a corner of the room. I was too young to care for the fandango. Of course, all this happened after work.

Departure to California 1912

By 1912, some people had enough money to buy passage on the ship to California, so they started to come. So, by that time, my father had sold the crop of sugar cane and the other two places and had enough money for the ship passage and some left over for expenses in a strange country. We didn't know anything about California. All we knew was that it grew wheat, grapes and all the things that grew in the old country.

My father, very serious, asked me, "Do you know how to say wheat in English? Also, other things in English, because, when we get there, we will have to find work."

I was only twelve years old.

So, on July 1, 1912, my father hired a horse and wagon and took us to Hilo, Hawaii with the old trunk and blankets. He also bought us a pair of shoes. That night he rented a room for us to sleep. That night, there was the first flushing toilet I had ever seen.

With us were my father's cousin's wife and five kids. They slept in the hall of the hotel. They didn't have any money, so my father put them in the room with us and we, the kids, slept on the floor.

The next morning we all went to a small harbor in Hilo and got on the same small ship that brought us to Hilo on the first trip, by the name Clodin. As we boarded the ship, the grocery store owners were there. We had nothing to fear, but my father's cousin's wife did not pay their grocery bill. She only had enough to pay the passage to Honolulu where her husband was waiting, so the store owners knocked her down and kicked her on deck. They were Portuguese.

Soon we were settled on deck, and the ship started moving toward Honolulu. That night we stopped by the island of Maui and picked up some chickens. The following day we reached Honolulu. My father's cousin was waiting for us there. He had two rooms rented for us for one week, while we waited for the big S.S. Wilhelmina, to take us to San Francisco, California. So, my folks went to the immigration building in Honolulu and got our clearance papers. We stayed more than three years, as was required on the papers that my father signed in Spain before we came.

So on July 12, 1912, we all got aboard the S.S. Wilhelmina. The Hawaiian band played "Aloha", when the ship started to move. Everybody got sea sick the first day, except my father. The second day I was around. The back deck of the ship was loaded with bananas. There on the ship, I ate my first dried prunes and ice cream. The voyage was very smooth all the way.

The 146 passenger S.S. Wilhelmina operated between San Francisco and Honolulu from 1910 to 1917. https://en.wikipedia.org/wiki/USS_Wilhelmina_ (ID-2168)

On July 17, 1912, at daybreak, we were going through the golden gate.

It was dark; all we could see were a few lights. The ship went to Pier No. 8, south of the ferry building. We were all ready to get off the ship, when my father and his cousin, by the name of Juan Lopez, each had a ship blanket underneath their arms. And then they glanced over the railings and saw the inspectors, checking everything, so they threw the blankets overboard on the other side of the ship.

We got off the ship and had the trunk and old blankets on the pier.

A delivery wagon man came to us and said,

"Where you want to go?"

We said, "Vacaville, California."

He said, "You have to go to the ferry building and get a boat to take you across to Oakland 16th Street and get on a train there."

So he charged two dollars to each family and disappeared.

After a long wait and everybody was hungry, a policeman approached us and said, "What is wrong?"

We told him the story with my English at that time. In ten minutes he was back with the fellow that took our money and was very drunk. So the policeman told him to take our luggage to the ferry building and we got on the ferry boat and went to Oakland. At 3 p.m., we were on 16th Street. At 4 p.m. we got on the train to Vacaville. We arrived there at 6 p.m. All this happened the same day we reached San Francisco. That was also my first train ride.

Before I forget, it was very cold in San Francisco that morning. And very hot in Vacaville. So my father and I started to walk toward town, a very small town at the time. About two blocks away, we met a family that we knew in Camp 4, Hamaulo.

He said, "That's the way I like to see friends go by."

He was very glad to see us.

He also said, "There is a vacant house next to mine."

So my father rented it. We slept that night there. Mind you, no furniture of any kind. Just the old trunk and the blankets. We lived in Vacaville for 2 months. My father worked in an orchard close to town picking plums and apricots for $1.50 a day for ten hours work. At night I used to go and see the show for a nickel, watching Indians and cowboys.

California 1912-1926:

Later a farmer from Fairfield, California needed help to harvest his apricots. He came to Vacaville for us in his automobile. I didn't know what make it was. It had brass all over, long straps tied to the headlights, gear shift on the outside. That was my first automobile ride, on a dirt road. There were no paved roads in California at that time.

When we got finished with this man's crop, we started to look for more work, walking from orchard to orchard on foot. I was the interpreter. Twelve years, wearing shoes, not used to walking miles and miles. Finally we got a prune orchard and stayed until everything was finished. All the while my father's cousin and his family were with us. After we finished picking prunes, the grower took all of us on his wagon to the Suisun railroad station. My father's cousin and family left for Santa Rosa, California to pick hops. We stayed in Fairfield three days looking for work.

They were laying the foundation for the present courthouse. My father couldn't speak English, so didn't get the job, so away we went to Santa Rosa too. My father's cousin had disappeared away. We knew a family from the same plantation in Hawaii, so we looked them up. They lived on 7th Street. The number I do not remember. We stayed a few days with them. Finally we rented a two room apartment, very old. My father got a job in the cannery, so did my mother. And I stayed home taking care of my two sisters,

Laura (10 years) and Rosie (5). My folks worked until the month of November, 1912, then they went to work in Sebastopol, California in the apple cannery.

We lived in a tent in the month of December in California. After the apple season was over, we went back to Santa Rosa to the same apartment and lived there until the spring of 1913.

By the way, I went to school in Santa Rosa. I enrolled at Lincoln school. The first day I took my slate that I had brought with me from Hawaii. The kids all laughed at the slate.

The first day the teacher gave some tests and put me in the first grade. In Hawaii, I was in the third grade. What a difference. That winter I was promoted to the third grade. I was very good at arithmetic and spelling. Also, that winter was our first Christmas on the mainland and I saw the first Christmas tree in my life. That winter my father wanted to go back to Hawaii, where he had a steady job, a home and everything else. Finally, he got a job with some other men, pruning grape vines in a little town north of Santa Rosa by the name Geyserville. There he changed his mind of going back to Hawaii again.

In 1913, I was going to grammar school in Santa Rosa, California. I was in the 3rd grade then. My neighbors were Italians and the kids got me to go to Catholicism school for one hour after grammar school from 3 p.m. to 4 p.m. Everything went fine for a few months, until I had to take Holy Communion. So one Saturday, I had to confess to the priest my sins. I didn't know what to say, so I said, "Forgive me father, I stole a few things." That's all I could remember, so he asked me, "Do you play around with little girls." At that time I didn't know what he meant. At that age I didn't know what sex was. So the next morning on Sunday, I went with the other boys to church and sat there with them. They told me to go in front where the priest is and finish your communion. I didn't move from my seat, and didn't go to Catholicism school any more. Up to today, I only go to church for weddings and funerals.

In March 1913, there was a family living near us by the name of Antonio Guerrero. Some of their children are still living in Sunnyvale, California by the names of Valverde and Bravo. This man, Antonio took a contact to grow hops west of Santa Rosa, and gave my father a job growing hops. We lived in a little one-room shack. There on April 28, 1913, my sister Mary was born. I went to a one-room schoolhouse and had to walk three miles each way.

That summer vacation time the boss gave me a job cutting the suckers off the hop vines and paid me one dollar a day. I worked from 7 a.m. to 6 p.m., ten hours a day. From there we went to Sebastopol with some other families and picked blackberries. We didn't make much money there.

After that, Antonio Guerrero and his family and also us went to Geyserville, California to harvest the grapes and prunes he pruned last winter. After that we all went back to Santa Rosa, lived there all winter. The Ojeda family lived there too. Art Ojeda, John Santaella, and myself used to distribute bills or programs and the manager gave us free passes for the show. In November that winter, my father, and Tony Ojeda and three other men had a contract to cut firewood in the town of Cloverdale, California. They had no interpreter to speak English, so my father took me out of school and I went with them to cut wood. The work was too hard for me, so they put me stacking wood.

At the end of 1913, after we finished the wood cutting, I went to school again and the teacher gave my father holy hell for getting me out of school.

Next spring, 1914, my father, and a man by the name of Antonio Cano and his family, also two other single men, went to work in a hop ranch one mile north of Hopland, California. We lived in tents and it rained a lot that year. We worked for a month. I was getting one dollar a day for ten hours, so was Philip Cano, one of the sons of Antonio Cano. We got along pretty good together.

Payday came along and there was no money for us. We worked for a California Indian, who had the contract to grow hops, and we worked for him; but he had a charge account in a grocery store in Hopland and the store owner took all of the money that the Indian owed him. So that left us holding the bag. We wouldn't work anymore until we got paid, so we went to see the district attorney in Ukiah. Philip Cano and his father, my father and me, and one of the single men started one afternoon walking from Hopland to Ukiah by railroad track. When it got dark we built a fire and slept under an oak tree. Mind you, no food of any kind. By 9 o'clock that morning, we reached Ukiah, saw the D.A. and explained everything to him. He told us to take a turnip and cut it and see if any blood comes out. Also said take anything the Indian has. He had a horse and wagon.

After, we walked back to Hopland; but before we left Ukiah, my father bought a loaf of bread and some cheese and had a bite to eat. Then we walked back to Hopland. The last few miles I could barely make it. My feet were sore and I was very tired. I slept for two days and nights.

Next thing we did; all men got on the wagon, started for Santa Rosa; and the women and children went by train. It took the men two days to get there.

In the meantime, one of my father's cousins, named Anna Salazar, came from Hilo, Hawaii. She was in Sebastopol cannery working apricots.

My father found out through some friends in Santa Rosa

that his cousin had sold our house in the sugar plantation for one hundred dollars and four dollars for the stove.

So my father decided to buy the horse and wagon and offered twenty seven dollars for the deal. Everybody was satisfied with the price. My father didn't pay the other people's share of the money until the next morning. His cousin was bringing money then. That night somebody else offered thirty dollars on the deal. My father said, "I was first, it is not fair. Everybody was satisfied with the deal, except the two single men." That night we went to stay in Chris Santaella's house on Third Street in Santa Rosa. Next day my father got the money from his cousin and went to take possession of the horse and wagon, the single men already had sold it to the buyer for thirty dollars. My father didn't like it, so some unpleasant words were exchanged. Then the younger man took a swing at my father and knocked him down. He was a husky fellow. So the second fellow went after my dad. I grabbed a stick that was laying by and hit the older man on the head. By that time, the young man came after my father again. I didn't know this; my father had a razor in his hand as the man came toward him. My father swung with the razor and cut his arm. Soon the police came, and one gallon of wine that was almost empty, they took them all to jail, including my father. Next day they had the trial and that afternoon, everybody was turned loose. We didn't get the horse and wagon.

Two days later we went with my father's cousin and family on the train to San Lorenzo, California to work in the cannery, but, there was no work to be had. In the meantime, news came that hops pickers were needed in Wheatland, California, a little town north of Roseville, California. So a few families, including three of my father's cousins and their families. We lived in tents. It was very hot. We picked hops for a week, then trouble started. A radical group called I.W.W. picketed the hops fields, so a few families and us left for another hop field in a place called Nord, fifteen miles north of Chico, California.

When we got there, they had too much help already, so we went to Chico and found work picking almonds and prunes. The orchard name was Tom Styles Ranch, which many years later my wife Josephine, her family and Harold Romero's family worked in the same ranch. After we finished harvesting the prunes, we went to Chico. All the time on foot, no transportation what so ever.

We stopped by the railroad depot. There was a Spanish man, by the name of José Galiano, who worked in the railroad depot park. My dad spoke to him and asked how things were around here. He said they needed men to work in the railroad section gang. Also that there was a vacant house two blocks from the depot.

So my father waited there until the section gang came. There was another Spanish man working there. So Dad asked for the job in his broken English. He got it. The foreman was a mean Irish man.

The next day we moved to the vacant house and my father went to work. This same house was where my daughter, Mary Gass, was born many years afterward. This was still 1914.

Every spring my father stopped working for the railroad and went to Nord to grow hops and pick prunes in summer. And school in the winter for me. This went on for the next four years.

In the fall of 1914, my sister Laura and I went to Rosedale school three blocks from home. That winter, I graduated to the 4th grade. There was another boy in the same grade with me. He was two years older than I. He was very good in math, but very poor in reading and writing. His name was Manuel Moreno. He started selling vegetables in an old car in the town of Alviso, California. In a few years he bought an old house on Washington Street in Sunnyvale, California and turned part of the house into a grocery store and lived in the other part. He had a large family. In a few years enlarged the store and bought a lot of old houses. He became one of the wealthiest men in Sunnyvale.

In the spring of 1915, the family started for the hops in Nord, California. The hop ranch was a very large place and also had a large camping ground. There I worked for a dollar a day for 10 hours growing hops. That took from March to July. Then we picked hops for 1 cent a pound. After that we went to Chico and picked prunes. That summer we were resting in the park by the railroad station when a train with the Liberty Bell, the cracked one, stopped there and everybody celebrated.

That summer a lot of Spanish people came to Chico to pick fruit and almonds. We still lived in the same house we rented the year before. One evening, the Romero family, Virginia's father and uncle, came walking up 5th Street from the depot. They spoke to my father and then they all went to the depot and got their things. They stayed in our house that night and a few more nights. Virginia was not in America yet. John Romero had his first wife then, a very nice woman with red hair. She had four girls and one boy. Most of the girls looked like her. She died in 1918 during the flu. That summer we all worked in Tom Style's ranch, three miles north of Chico. We lived in tents. There Aurora Romero was born, John Romero's daughter. She died in 1931 in a cannery.

That fall I went to school again. I graduated to the 5th grade. I was behind the rest of the kids, but the teacher helped me to catch up. I was very good at math and spelling.

That winter, we moved to a bigger house on the corner of 9th and Cedar. Virginia's uncle, José, lived with us. I graduated to the 6th grade. After that I didn't go to school anymore. That spring we all went to the big hop ranch in Nord.

Some Hindu had the contract to grow hops, but the farmer hired us to help them. That year I got men's pay. I had to work hard to keep up with them. Also there were two Filipino boys. They showed me how to fish in the Sacramento River. After work we used to catch minnows and put them on larger hooks and line. We threw the line out in the river. Next morning there was striped bass or a pike fish hooked on the line. That summer, we had more fish than we could eat.

That year, in February, 1916, my little brother was born. His name was Manuel Lopez. He died in August while we were picking hops. He had sunstroke and died one month later.

That year my father bought me a woman's bicycle without brakes. All you could do is pedal forward and drag your feet to stop. That fall a Spanish boy and I went to look for work in the rice fields 30 miles away on our bikes. We came home the same day. I was very tired on my bike that needed continued pedaling. He used to coast on his.

By the way, that Spanish boy and his mother lived with us in the same house. His name was John Marquez. His sister was Belin. She lived in San Leandro, California. Her and her husband got killed in an accident and seven others. Going between San Francisco and San Leandro, California.

That year this boy, his mother and brother came to the hops field to work with us. They didn't stay long. His brother missed his wine and went back to Chico again. Also, that summer, just before hop picking, a lot of Spanish people came to pick hops. I met Ralph Gallardo, his brother Manuel; he was my age, and the rest of their family.

Also, a man by the name of José Perez Romero, who happened to be my future wife's uncle years later. He was a very pleasant man.

He had a round, dark face like Johnny Borrego. This was 1917. He died in 1919 in San Francisco with the flu.

After summer was over we all went to Chico. There I met a Spanish boy by the name of José Marquez. He was my age. He just arrived from Spain. His parents passed away and his uncle brought him to America. That fall we worked in a nursery. He couldn't speak one word in English and I couldn't speak very good Spanish. So we made a deal, every week day, after work, and supper we gathered at his uncle's house for two hours, from 7 until 9. He taught me Spanish and I taught him English. I caught on right away, for him it was harder.

He wanted to speak English very bad. His father was cabinet maker and he knew the trade. He was from a town, Valdepeñas, south of Madrid, Spain. The boy had a very good education in Spanish. When we were doing good in our education, the other boys wanted to come in with us. There were two fellows, very rough and uneducated, didn't know English or Spanish. I told Pepe their laughing and joking, we couldn't study.

Later Pepe got married to a Spanish girl from his part of the country and moved to Pittsburg, California, and worked for a large lumber company. He passed away in Pittsburg in 1972, as did John Marquez, Belin's brother.

On January 19, 1919, my brother Frank was born and my folks decided not to go and work in the hops fields that year. So he got a job for me on the railroad section gang with him, getting 40 cents an hour. I was only 18 years at the time. It was hard work. I weighed 163 pounds when I went to work there and only 141 pounds when I came out. A few days later my father and I got a job in the Diamond Match Factory yard digging ditches for a water line. One day the head foreman came by and said "Come in, I will give you a job."

I did go. He put me in the machine shop at 50 cents an hour. That was great for the year 1920.

I worked there for a few months. I liked it very much, but soon my father got restless, so we bought a 1917 overland car, a pile of junk. All it would go was 30 miles per hour. The speed limit was 25 miles then. There were very few good roads. Anyway I quit my job to help the folks. Back to prunes and hops again. In 1923, in the spring, we all went to New Castle, California to pick plums and peaches, and my sisters, Laura and Rose, packed the fruit in crates to be shipped back east.

My father made a lot of money that year. There in Rocklin, we met the Morales family that came with us from Spain. They played a big part in our lives.

In the spring of 1924, we took a contract to grow hops south of Oroville, California and made good money there. Then we went to Chico again. I forgot to say my folks bought a house in Chico in 1920. It was on 951 Walnut Street next to Chico Creek and a few houses away lived an American family with two girls. The oldest girl was married to a Portuguese man. She used to call him black Portuguese and very foul language; and the young one came after me. I didn't say this before; I was very girl shy and did not like this girl. She was too loose and too fast, so I stayed away from her. She got in trouble later.

In 1924, after we came from the hops field in Oroville, there was a Spanish girl working in the Diamond Match factory by the name of Josephine Galiano. She was the daughter of José Galiano who worked in the Southern Pacific depot park. She was born in Melilla, Spanish Morocco. Like Carmen Diaz, they came in the same ship we did. Anyway, her cousin was married to Joe Flores, a friend of mine, also my age. So one day he and I were walking to town. He said, "Why don't you speak to Josie, she has no boyfriend."

I was very shy. Then he said, "Tomorrow, Sunday, Mary, my wife and I will go to the park with Josie and you speak to her." So the next day I walked to the park. I was ashamed to drive the old junk.

They were waiting for me, so we talked and walked around the park. I had known her for many years, but never paid any attention to her. She was very small and good looking. I fell over heels over her. Things went pretty good until Ralph Gallardo, my wife's cousin (the one that is married to Virginia), began to cut in and she left me out. I didn't interfere with her any more.

So, a few months went by and they broke up. Then she sent a note with my sister, she wanted to see me. So I met her on the way to work and everything was O.K. She said, "Speak to my father and see what he says." I did the following day. That was the custom those days. He told me he was taking his family back to Spain and if he changed his mind, it was alright.

Just think, I was 24 years and she was 21 years. Things went pretty smooth, then one day she told me, "I am not going to Spain." What better hint does a fellow want? I didn't do nothing.

Things went as usual until the spring of 1925. Her family went to cut asparagus down by Isleton, California and I went to Los Molinos, California in the hops fields and worked there all summer and never went once to see her. I was too timid for my folks and her father.

She suffered a lot cutting asparagus like men. They met a family by the name Guzman, and they all went to live in San Leandro, California and never came back to Chico. She married Joe Guzman, a nice boy. She later told Virginia Gallardo that I didn't go and see her while she was cutting asparagus. By the way, Ralph Gallardo married Virginia. They now live in Hayward, California

In the meantime, 1926, Harold Romero had an older sister named Rose. She was very dark complected. Her folks used to dress her up, powder her face and come to our house with her. I used to sneak out the back door, went to town with the boys. So, they got angry with us and didn't come anymore. That summer my folks and I went to New Castle, California and work in the fruit. After summer, we went back to Chico.

Marriage and Family 1926-1935

In the summer of 1926, the Borrego family appeared in Chico. Antonio Borrego took his family to pick prunes and the last thing they picked was olives in Olinda, California, south of Redding. They moved to Chico and came to live next door to us. There I met Josie, which is my wife today.

Her father was very strict with her, didn't let her go anywhere except to work in the Diamond Match factory. She was not 16 years of age, but looked 19 years. I didn't believe that she was that young. I proposed to her by notes, so her father wouldn't get suspicious. This went on for two months. She told me she was very unhappy at home. Her father using the money she earned in the factory for making booze. He mistreated her mother and brothers. One day I asked her, "Would you like to get married?" She hesitated for a couple of days, then she agreed to elope with me.

Before this, one raining day, I decided to pick her up and bring her one block away from home. Her father decided the same thing, so I got there first with my Buick car. We were coming home when we spotted her father with the Ford truck on the crossroads. He couldn't see us with those curtains on the truck.

She ducked under the seat and we went by. Later he asked her where she had been. She told him, "I came with the Portuguese girl that worked there."

On January 27, 1927, we decided to elope. One day before that, I asked my mother for the three hundred dollars that the Morales family paid us a few days before. We had loaned it to them a few months before. My mother gave me the money and that night I took my suit of clothes and put it under the back seat of the car. The next morning I pushed the car out of the garage. Nobody knew anything besides my mother.

I drove up to the factory and didn't see Josie, a few seconds later she came out of the office. She had me scared for a while. She got in the car and we headed for Rocklin where Frank Morales' family lived. They were surprised to see us. Then we went to the place Frank Morales was working in New Castle, also a surprise for him. Frank Morales and his wife went with us to Auburn, California and got our marriage license. Then we all went to Roseville to a Catholic Church and the priest opened the church at 4 P.M. and married us all in one day.

Before we went to church, Josie had to buy some clothes. All she had was a working dress and a pair of old shoes. Also, we bought the ring.

At 6 p.m. the same day, we sent her father a telegram telling him to forgive us for what we did. When he got it, he went wild. He threw all Josie's clothes and shoes down the creek that went by. He grabbed little Johnny Borrego, opened the wood heater, was going to throw him in, but Josie's mother held his arm. The next day he disappeared from Chico. We came to Chico in five days and lived with my folks. That "was my first mistake".

My sister Laura got married in February 1927 and my father gave me another one hundred dollars the day my sister got married.

That spring we all went to Los Molinos and grew hops. We had a contract to grow the darn things. We split it five ways: two ways for my wife and me and three ways for my folks.

By that time Josie was pregnant and she worked hard like the rest of us and we saved some money. That fall we went back to Chico and picked prunes. My wife was too big and she stayed home. But during the day she went to see her *paisanos* on 5th Street. There they put some funny ideas in her mind. Also there were Harold Romero's mother and sister, Rose.

A few days later my folks and I went to work early in the morning, and when we came back the dirty dishes were in the sink. I knew there was something wrong. She changed her ways, so right after that we rented a house on 5th Street next to her *paisanos*. We bought some nude furniture. I painted it myself. I also went to work in the rice fields. I had my father's car to get around.

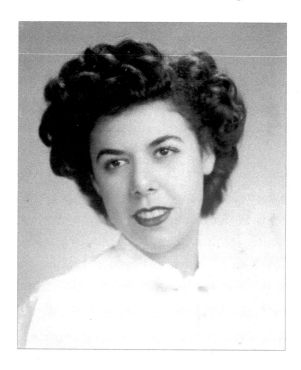

On October 23, 1927 my daughter Mary was born. We had Doctor Johnson, the best for these cases.

That winter we went to Los Molinos and pruned trees and grape vines. My father came along with us and my wife cooked and washed our clothes. It was very cold that winter. It got to 17 above. The next spring, 1928, we went to New Castle and worked in the fruit on a Japanese ranch and they taught Josie how to pack fruit in crates. My folks also went to New Castle and worked in the fruit with my sister Laura, on a different ranch.

The following year, 1929, after we worked the fruit in New Castle, we went back to Chico to rent a house, one block away from where Mary was born. I went to pick olives with the Romero's in Oroville, California. I did my own cooking and lived by myself. One Saturday when I went to Chico to get clean clothes.

That night my son, Tony, was born (November 20, 1929). He did not have a doctor. Some friends acted as midwives. Mother and son were doing very good.

After that we continued pruning in the winter and picking fruit in the summer. In the fall of 1930, my brother-in-law, Tony Borrego was living in Mountain View, California. His father and family lived with him on Washington Street. He wrote to us telling us to come down. His father said everything is forgiven. We hadn't seen Josie's family since we eloped, so we came down and everything was O.K.

That night Tony, his wife, Connie Borrego, and ourselves, went to San Jose to see a show. When we came back, Josie's father was sick and drunk. He made her mother cook some chorizos and drank a lot of wine that made him very mean. He was going to beat us all up, then got sick and was laying there in a bed.

The next day I asked Tony if he wanted to come and prune with me and he said he would. He had no job and some unpaid bills, so he went to Los Molinos, California and worked. We were getting 50 cents an hour. In a few days he said he would like to bring his grandfather and grandmother. I said, "Sure, bring them. We have plenty of room here."

Tony's grandfather and grandmother were Jose Perez Lopez and Teresa Romero Tecero.

They immigrated to Hawaii on the second voyage of the Willesden in 1913 and later moved to California.

We had a long cabin with 8 rooms, 2 rooms to a family; rent free, also water and light. So they all stayed in the ranch five months. He paid all his bills and went back to wash asparagus.

We went back to New Castle for the summer work. About July 1931, we received a telegram that Tony's father was dead. We rushed to Vacaville where the family lived. He had committed suicide. He was in debt to the gills, had no work and couldn't support the family. So he shot himself with a shotgun.

There was no money for the burial. Tony, my brother-in-law, paid the bill. Then I paid 1/3 of the cost and Teresa, the other sister, paid the other 1/3. After that, my family and I went back to work in New Castle. Later back to Los Molinos again.

Before I forget, the last summer we picked prunes we had my son, Tony, out in the orchard inside a lug box. He was a year old. He reached over the side of the box, picked up dirt and ate it. Little Mary was always riding on the fruit wagons going to the drying yard.

By that time the depression came and was getting worse every day. In 1932, we went to New Castle to work in the fruit, getting only 15 cents an hour, and lucky to get that. By late summer it got real bad. I received 12 ½ cents per hour for pruning.

My daughter Josie was born that year on October 21, 1932. A premature baby. We had a rough time with her. She was rupture, had to be operated.

By the way, in 1929 I bought a used Chevrolet car and gave the Buick back to my father. The family was not getting along at all. My mother was not an easy person to get along with. My wife was a good mother and a good wife, but she is no angel. We separated from my folks. I went to live in Gerber, California and my folks stayed in Los Molinos. We all worked for the same company (Clemens Horst Company).

In the spring of 1935, we received a telegram saying Joe Borrego had died. We rushed to Mountain View for the funeral. Joe was only 18 years old. He and some other boys took a ride on the train from Mountain View to Sunnyvale and they jumped the train before it stopped. Joe jumped on the wrong side of the tracks, in the path of another train going the other way. The casket was closed at the wake.

After all this was over, Josie's sister, Teresa, talked my wife into coming to work in the cannery, so we went back to Gerber. We loaded our things on a little trailer and car and came to Isleton, California to work in the asparagus cannery. After that we came to Alviso, California and worked on apricots and pears.

After the season was over we loaded our things on the trailer and got ready to go back to Isleton and work the tomatoes.

Before we left, we came to Mountain View to say goodbye. Tony Borrego proposed to me to stay in the gas station he was running. I said I would on a 50/50 basis. He hesitated for a while and later said okay. I stayed.

California Migrant Work
of Joseph Lopez and Family
1912-1935

Compiled by Susan Burkholder

City	Crop or Job
Vacaville	Plums, Apricots
Fairfield	Apricots, Prunes
Santa Rosa	Hops, Cannery
Sebastopol	Blackberries, Cannery
Geyserville	Pruning Grape Vines, Grapes, Prunes
Cloverdale	Firewood
Hopland	Harvesting Hops
Wheatland	Harvesting Hops
Chico	Almonds, Prunes, Road Section Gang
Nord	Hops
Chico	Diamond Match Factory, Digging Ditches , Machine Shop
New Castle	Plums, Peaches
Oroville	Olives, Growing Hops
Los Molinas	Harvesting Hops, Pruning Trees and Grape Vines
Isleton	Asparagus, Tomatoes, Cannery
Alviso	Apricots, Pears

Welder, Machinist, Gas Station Owner

I had $800 which we used to buy a hoist for lubricating cars and $500 worth of tires and tubes for resale. Things went pretty well for two months, then one day Tony told me General Petroleum Company didn't like me, so he laid me off. So there I was no money, no job. I wrote to Los Molinos for a job and I didn't get an answer for two weeks. Tony told me to come back on my own and all the money I made in lubrication, tires, batteries and tire repairs was mine and all the money from gas and oil was his. I was not too happy with the deal, but left me no choice, so I stuck it out. Just barely making a living.

The wife had to work in the cannery so we could live. It went on like this until Pearl Harbor days, then all the men between 18 to 45 years of age were drafted for service.

Both Tony and I went to Palo Alto welding school. Then one day Tony went to work in a South San Francisco shipyard. I took care of the gas station. Oh, I forgot, when the war started, Tony took the whole station profits and paid me $32 a week. He also paid me $400 of the original. He worked in the shipyard three nights, then he quit his job and told me to go try it.

I took the welding test and passed. I worked in the shipyard in San Francisco for 18 months. Then I quit the shipyard. The foreman said, "You will be sorry. We are going to put you in A-1 at the draft board." I didn't care. I already had a job as a machinist at Westinghouse in Sunnyvale. I worked there until the 31st day of December, 1944. Tony Borrego sold me the gas station a week before for $2,000. There was nothing there. I took inventory on January 2, 1945. There was the hoist, a little gas and a few ration gas stamps. Tony said Don Luis offered $2,000, but that he would give me first chance, so I took it. After a few weeks later the Mobil Oil Company officers came around and asked me how I got the station.

I told them I was paying Tony $2,000 for it. They said he cannot do that. The station is owned and controlled by Mobil Oil. All he can sell is the stock and old equipment. Goodwill is 10 cents a dozen. I told them to go and talk to Tony. They did. He didn't like it at all. He got angry with me too. He said, "A deal is a deal".

I told him that when I sell the station all I can sell is the stock. That is all I did when I sold it to Johnny Borrego when he bought me out.

During the next nine months I didn't make much money. We were living and making payments on a house we bought at 536 Hope Street. We bought it for $2,300 with the kid's piggy bank money and some of our own savings.

When the war ended in 1945, I started to make money. I paid the mortgage off.

Before I forget, my brother Frank Lopez was drafted into service and my sister Mary Rios brought my parents to Sunnyvale.

My father died in August 1945 of cancer of the throat. He suffered 14 months with the sickness. It was horrible. My mother went to live with Frank, my brother in Sunnyvale, after he was discharged from the service. He worked for me for two years and then went to work for Libby's cannery. He is still there today.

Josephine Lopez opened a gift shop on Hope Street in Mountain View, CA

Manual Lopez Bilbao, Joseph Lopez Lopez, Maria Lopez Diaz

I knew I was forgetting something. In 1935, while I was in the gas station with Tony, a lot of Spanish young men decided to become American citizens. We went to San Jose, California for some applications and some books to study the constitution. We also applied to the immigration building in Hawaii. Everybody got their answer, except me. They couldn't find mine, so I had to register again in the federal building in San Francisco with two witnesses, Joe Diaz and Joe Gonzales. I had to wait five years for my final papers.

I explained this to my parents. They said there was a reason. Before we came to Hawaii, my father got in trouble with the Spanish police. He and some other men were making charcoal in the forest, against the law. The police fired but missed. Then they, in turn, threw stones at them and knocked one of the police's gun off his hand. But they got away. The police never found out who they were.

My father said that there was no work and they had to make a living, so he came to Hawaii with his cousin's papers. So, I came here with a different name, Antonio Rosillo. Everybody else came with a different name. I never mentioned this to nobody until now. I didn't get my citizen papers until July 20, 1940.

Ship	Page	Line	Surname	Name	Age	Sex	Status	Residence in Spain
Heliopolis	89	1	Salazar Molina	ANTONIO SALAZAR MOLINA	42	M	M	IZBOR DEL RIO (GRANADA)
Heliopolis	89	2	Lopez Bilbao	ANA LOPEZ BILBAO	40	F	M	IZBOR DEL RIO (GRANADA)
Heliopolis	89	3	Salazar Lopez	MARIA JOSEFA SALAZAR LOPEZ	18	F	S	IZBOR DEL RIO (GRANADA)
Heliopolis	89	4	Salazar Lopez	ANTONIO SALAZAR LOPEZ	13	M	S	IZBOR DEL RIO (GRANADA)
Heliopolis	89	5	Salazar Lopez	FRANCISCA	7	F	S	IZBOR DEL RIO (GRANADA)
Heliopolis	89	6	Salazar Lopez	ANA	3	F	S	IZBOR DEL RIO (GRANADA)
Heliopolis	89	7	Salazar Lopez	JUAN	10mo	M	S	IZBOR DEL RIO (GRANADA)
Heliopolis	89	8	Morales Lopez	GASPAR MORALES LOPEZ	27	M	M	IZBOR DEL RIO (GRANADA)
Heliopolis	89	9	Cobos Villalba	ISABEL COBOS VILLALBA	27	F	M	IZBOR DEL RIO (GRANADA)
Heliopolis	89	10	Morales Cobos	FRANCISCO	5	M	S	IZBOR DEL RIO (GRANADA)
Heliopolis	89	11	Morales Cobos	MIGUEL	1	M	S	IZBOR DEL RIO (GRANADA)
Heliopolis	89	12	Lopez Morales	ANTONIO LOPEZ MORALES	36	M	M	IZBOR DEL RIO (GRANADA)
Heliopolis	89	13	Rosillo Morillo	MARIA ROSILLO MORILLO	35	F	M	IZBOR DEL RIO (GRANADA)
Heliopolis	89	14	Lopez Rosillo	ANTONIO	8	M	S	IZBOR DEL RIO (GRANADA)
Heliopolis	89	15	Lopez Rosillo	JOSEFA	5	F	S	IZBOR DEL RIO (GRANADA)
Heliopolis	89	16	Lopez Exposito	MANUEL LOPEZ EXPOSITO	26	M	M	IZBOR DEL RIO (GRANADA)
Heliopolis	89	17	Alvarez Jimenez	CARMEN ALVAREZ JIMENEZ	23	F	M	IZBOR DEL RIO (GRANADA)
Heliopolis	89	18	Lopez Alvarez	ANTONIO	2	M	S	IZBOR DEL RIO (GRANADA)
Heliopolis	89	19	Lopez Alvarez	CARMEN	1	F	S	IZBOR DEL RIO (GRANADA)
Heliopolis	89	20	Lopez Bilbao	JUAN LOPEZ BILBAO	34	M	M	IZBOR DEL RIO (GRANADA)
Heliopolis	89	21	Salazar Rodriguez	ANTONIA SALAZAR RODRIGUEZ	34	F	M	IZBOR DEL RIO (GRANADA)
Heliopolis	89	22	Lopez Salazar	ANTONIO	10	M	S	IZBOR DEL RIO (GRANADA)
Heliopolis	89	23	Lopez Salazar	JOSE	8	M	S	IZBOR DEL RIO (GRANADA)
Heliopolis	89	24	Lopez Salazar	JUAN	2	M	S	IZBOR DEL RIO (GRANADA)
Heliopolis	89	25	Lopez Bilbao	ANTONIO LOPEZ BILBAO	37	M	M	IZBOR DEL RIO (GRANADA)
Heliopolis	89	26	Exposito	MARIA EXPOSITO	31	F	M	IZBOR DEL RIO (GRANADA)
Heliopolis	89	27	Lopez Exposito	EDUARDO	9	M	S	IZBOR DEL RIO (GRANADA)
Heliopolis	89	28	Lopez Exposito	MANUEL	5	M	S	IZBOR DEL RIO (GRANADA)
Heliopolis	89	29	Lopez Exposito	ANTONIO	2	M	S	IZBOR DEL RIO (GRANADA)

These are the 29 people (Six Families) who traveled to Hawaii on the S.S. Heliopolis from Izbor del Rio.

- Joseph Lopez Lopez traveled under the name Antonio Rosillo (#14).
- With him were his sister Delores (Laura) traveling under the name Josefa Lopez Rosillo (#15)
- His father, traveling under the name Antonio Lopez Morales (#12)
- His mother, traveling under the name Maria Rosillo Morillo (#13).
- Ana Lopez Bilbao (#2), her husband, and their 5 children would have been Joseph Lopez's paterna aunt, uncle by marriage and his first cousins.
- Juan Lopez Bilbao (#20), his wife, and their 3 children would have been Joseph Lopez's paterna uncle, aunt by marriage and his first cousins.
- Antonio Lopez Bilbao (#25), his wife, and their 3 children would have been Joseph Lopez's paterna uncle, aunt by marriage and his first cousins.
- Based on other family documents, it is highly likely that the Lopez Alvarez family (#16-19) was also related to Joseph Lopez Lopez.
- Given the Lopez name, and the small size of Izbor del Rio, even the Lopez Morales Cobos family (#8 #11) were probably related as well.

Return to Spain 1949

On March 15, 1949, my wife and I and four other couples went to Spain on a TWA prop job.

Two hundred miles from Kansas City, Missouri, one motor caught fire. The pilot radioed in to Kansas City and they had another plane ready for us. Then we stopped in Chicago and last New York City. We stayed there two days to see the sights, then to Spain. We reached Madrid about 5:30 p.m. It was 11 p.m. before we got to the hotel. The next day it was very cold. In Madrid, we stayed three days; then went on the train to Málaga. There, Joe Diaz's cousin was supposed to exchange dollars for pesetas – 32 pesetas for a dollar on the black market. The regular exchange was 25 pesetas for a dollar. But Joe Diaz's cousin was not in Málaga. He was in Tangiers, North Africa.

By the way, my wife and the other women snuck 500 dollars cash to exchange on the black market.

[Susan Burkholder 2017. Montellano]

We stayed in Málaga three days. The village I was born in was not too far away; but we decided to go to Montellano, Sevilla on the train.

We reached Utera, a good town, not too far away from Montellano, about 6 P.M. and got a taxi. Ralph Gallardo, Virginia, and us in one taxi. Tony got one for him and his wife.

It was dark by the time we reached the town. It is a good sized place. The next day, with a few of my wife's relatives – the men folks – we walked 8 kilometers (about 4 miles) to a farm where my wife's cousin worked. The women went on a truck. They also had a house in town.

I drank some water from a spring in the farm and got the dysentery, and no bathroom anywhere. I was sick for a few days.

Then we left for Granada with Virginia and Ralph Gallardo. Virginia has a brother that lives in Atarfe, provincia of Granada. I had an aunt, her husband and son living in the same town. They were very poor. This aunt was my mother's sister. The next day, I gave them 300 pesetas that my mother gave me for them.

[Encarus Lopez Alvarez (granddaughter of Josefa Lopez Chavez met Susan Burkholder, (granddaughter of Joseph Lopez Lopez) in Izbor, Spain in October 2017]

This was April 1, 1949. We went to the city of Granada, my wife and I all alone. Everybody else stayed in their home towns. The same day at 5 P.M. we left Granada for the village of my birth, on an old bus. The driver left us by the road, by a steep hill instead of taking us to the *parador*. Anyway, my cousin, Josefa Lopez Chavez, saw us and came down to meet us. She and the kids carried the suitcases up the hill.

I was disappointed when I reached the old village; everything seemed smaller. Everybody turned out to see us. They were dressed very poor, we were dressed fairly well. As soon as we reached the place, I remembered my grandfather's house, the same one I was sleeping in that February 1907. We kept on walking. I told them where the water fountain was, also the church by the cemetery. I showed them the house where I was born. Only the stairs were not in the same place. The church and a few other houses had red tile roofs; the older houses were built Moorish style. We stayed there two days, then left for Granada on the road that we left on February 1907; only we went north instead of south to the Mediterranean Sea.

Photo of family in Spain. Notes on the back of the photo. Found amongst Josephine Lopez's photos. Unknown as to whether this is Izbor (Lopez relatives) or Montellano (Borrego relatives).

We rented a room in the Hotel Alameda for 50 pesetas a day – room and board - each about two dollars American money. We paid for these things, but didn't use them very much. We went often to Atarfe to where Virginia and Ralph were staying.

We also met my father's older sister's children, all grown up. They were tall and very fair people.

From there we went on a street car to Granada and saw the Alhambra, the palace of the Moors - flowers and fountains all over.

It was built 8 centuries ago and today is as pretty as the first years it was built and the Moors had it. There was half a million people there. By the way, there are many Moorish castles in Spain today. Granada is one of the pretty and clean cities of Spain, with a beautiful valley below that grows everything — cotton, tobacco and sugar beet. Back of the city are the Sierra Nevada Mountains, solid packed with snow, even in the summer time. The city has more water than they can use. It is not like some parts of Spain, hot and dry. It has a forest and green vegetation all over, that is why the Moors picked that place to build their palace. It is on a high cliff with only one entrance. There is also a tunnel from the Alhambra underneath (Rio Genil) the river, to the gypsy's quarters called Albaicín and Sacro-Monte.

My aunt that lived in Atarfe had two sons. The oldest boy was shot and killed by the police, the "Guardia Civil" the most hated police in Spain "Spanish Gestapo". The boy went to town and cut short through an olive grove walking. The police saw him and they shot him.

This special police traveled in pairs, one with a machine gun and the other with an automatic rifle. The police knew he had fought on the loyalist side, that is the republica side. This happened after the Civil War was over.

Virginia Gallardo went to Spain in March, 1978 and saw that my aunt was still living. The government had given her a lot of money for that incident.

On April 15, 1949, we left Granada and were going to Sevilla on the same day. Tony and the whole gang were coming from Sevilla to Granada, so the trains crossed each other.

It was night and raining when we got there. We took a horse and rig taxi to the hotel. A slick guy got in the taxi with us and he wanted to take us to another hotel, where he received a commission. We said no, we had our hotel picked out. He was fast, as we reached the hotel, he ran in and told the owners he had some customers and got a commission.

The owners later told me they gave him 5 pesetas a day for his troubles. That is one (Spanish dollars). In American money it was only 20 cents.

Sevilla is a very pretty city and bigger than Granada, very romantic. We missed Easter week, the best in the world; but saw "The Feria". There is nothing like it in Spain or anywhere in the world. They sing and dance for 24 hours a day for a whole week.

After that my wife's cousin, Anna, came to Sevilla and brought us the money from the exchange of the 500 dollars we brought with us. Tony Borrego and the others had gone to Tangiers and exchanged for pesetas, which amounted to 17,000 pesetas. We gave her 600 pesetas for her troubles. The next few days we saw two great bullfights in Sevilla.

One more thing, the region of Andalucía is considered the California of Spain, that is the eight *provincias* (provinces) of south Spain including Málaga, Granada and Sevilla.

On May 1, 1949, Ralph and Virginia Gallardo and us decided to come home, so we went to the travel agency to buy tickets for Madrid. They told us we had to wait seven days before we could go, so we went back to the hotel and told the owners what happened. He said, "No problem." He called the bellhop and told us to give the boy 50 pesetas plus railroad fare. We did. In a half hour the boy was back with our train tickets. Everything was black market.

On the 7th day of May, 1949, we left for Madrid. We went through "La Mancha". Nothing but wine grapes on both sides of the tracks. We reached Madrid at night. Another slick operator approached us in the train depot. He wanted to carry our luggage to the hotel. I said no. Another fellow carried our luggage to a taxi that carried a lot of people. We told the driver to take us to Hotel Christina.

I don't know he did it, but this fellow got to the hotel desk before we did to get a commission. These guy work fast. We stayed in Madrid a few days. Mr. Calvo, from Mountain View, California, gave me a movie camera to take to his nephew in Madrid to take pictures of the soccer ball field and other places we visited with Mr. Calvo's sister. They showed us some interesting places.

About the last part of May 1949, we left for home. We left Madrid airport Saturday at midnight; got to New York at 5 P.M. Sunday; waited three hours for a plane to California and reached San Francisco airport at 5 A.M. Monday morning. We called my daughter, Mary, to pick us up.

Tony Borrego and the others came in a month later. They went to Valencia and Tangiers, we didn't.

While we were away, my brother Frank Lopez took care of the gas station. Also, my son, Tony, and Art, Mary's husband; lived in our house while we were away.

Grandchildren, Real Estate, Orchards, and Vineyards

Everything went pretty smooth for a while. When I had the dysentery in Spain, I also had a fissure in my rectum that was bleeding. I had surgery in February 1950 and finally felt better and was doing real good at the gas station.

My grandson, Steve Gass, was one year old when we went to Spain and the grandmother bought him some foolish little things from there. Later my wife and I had a misunderstanding. I got stubborn and wouldn't speak to her. She went to see a lawyer and we were separated for three months. I didn't want a divorce. I got so stubborn. I didn't go back to make up. She did. I did not have interest in any other women, and in 1953 it happened again. This time she dumped my things in the pickup at the gas station. It lasted two months. I wouldn't give in, she did. From there on, no more silly stuff.

In 1954, my daughter Josie left the house; the mother and her had a little row. The mother was a little strict with her, so she left the house. Our son, Tony, left in July 1954, so that left the two of us.

After a few days some real estates wanted to buy our house and other properties nearby. They offered me nine thousand dollars. I told him he was crazy. The following week, he offered twelve thousand dollars, we said no. A few days later, fifteen thousand. I told him we want twenty thousand clear. He hesitated for a while. Finally he agreed on the price. We knew they wanted it for a shopping center. We bought a new house on Todd Street, Mountain View for fourteen thousand, five hundred dollars. The following year, we sold it for sixteen thousand, five hundred dollars and bought a nice home and a nice four-plex on Pettis Street for fifty five thousand dollars. I had to borrow twenty nine thousand dollars from Bank of America. In the meantime I joined the Masonic Lodge and on August 1957, my mother passed away. She had surgery of the liver. It was cancer. She was over 80 years old.

I am not sure of the date; but my daughter, Josie got married in 1954 to a boy named Russell Neal Hassinger. They lived in the Bay Area for a while, then moved to Sooner, Oklahoma. In May, 1955, Neal went to Sooner College and Josie worked while all this was going.

Josephine, (Russell) Neal, Josie, Joe

The Mobile Oil Company built a new gas station on the same location the old one was. Everything went good, making a good family living.

In June 1959, my wife went to Grand Junction, Colorado. Josie was going to have her first baby. The baby was born July 11, 1959. His name is Jerry. On Christmas 1959, my wife and grandson Steven, and I went to Grand Junction, then to Springfield, Colorado where Neal's family lived. We had a nice holiday there with them. In January, 1960 we came home. It was very cold there, a lot of snow.

Joe with his grandson, Jerry Hassinger

Joe's oldest grandson, Steve Gass with Jerry Hassinger

On July 1954, my son Tony Lopez got married to LaVida Davis, and on November 15, 1955, little Tony Lopez was born a premature baby. We thought he was not going to live, he was so little and weak. But he finally made it. He is the biggest one of the family today.

On March 15, 1957, Ronnie Lopez was born, a nice healthy boy; but he was never as big as his older brother Tony. He is already married and has a little baby girl, named Caprice. She was born on August 31, 1975; a very healthy baby.

On April 2, 1959, Terilynn Lopez was born. She is going to

college today. Next, following her; Lynette Lopez was born on June 16, 1960. She has her father's complexion, a nice looking girl. The last one of the family, a healthy baby boy, by the name of Michael Lopez; that at 16 years of age is almost as big as his brother, Tony Lopez, Jr. This includes all of Tony Lopez, Sr's, family.

While were living in the almond orchard in Escalon, California, Josie's little girl, Susan Hassinger, was born in Casper, Wyoming, on March 10, 1962. She is a nice young lady today. Also, in the same year Mary, my daughter's little boy was born on July 3, 1962. He is a very handsome boy, and very good looking. Only sometimes he gives his mother a bad time, but I think he will outgrow that.

During this time, the Mobil Oil Company built a new gas station on the same location that the old one was. Everything went well and I was making a fairly good living.

By the summer of 1958, I had a contractor build a duplex behind the four-plex on Pettis Street and borrowed more money from Bank of America.

In January 1961, I decide to buy an almond orchard in Ripon, California for fifty-five thousand dollars. It had 20 acres of almonds, one nice house and a tractor. I sold my property on Pettis Street for $87,500, but I still owed the bank a lot of money at the time. The real estate man bought my property without any money. He borrowed $53,000 to pay my bank loan and the rest of the money he gave me in a second deed of trust, which I used to buy the ranch at a very small monthly payment. I borrowed $15,000 from Central Bank in Ripon at 6% to pay for the ranch. The first year, I had a good crop of almonds. The second year was not so good. I was having a hard time paying the bank in Ripon. Mr. Bishop's, the man that bought my property on Pettis, second deed of trust notes were not paying enough. He owed me $13,000. He paid me $72 a year. Another mistake I made buying the darn ranch.

I spent a lot of money improving the place. The 1963 crop was not so good either. In August 1963 we sold the ranch to a Portuguese man from the Bay Area for $57,500 and moved to Mountain View again. We lived with my daughter Mary in the meantime. Mary was working for William Brothers Construction. They worked a good deal for me. They had a choice piece of property in Sunnyvale, California, big enough to build two four-plex apartments, complete with refrigerators and a lot of other things that went with it.

I needed a loan of $80,000 to build the apartments. John Williams took the second note from Mr. Bishop that owed me and $15,000 I had. This made up the $95,000 that was needed to build.

In the meantime, I had a Mobil Oil Gas Station on El Camino Real and Mary Avenue in Sunnyvale. The building went on nicely.

I worked the gas station, but was not making too much money. The station was on a bad corner and customers couldn't make the left turn into the station. I had it for a year then sold it back to Mobil Oil Company.

In the meantime, the apartments were finished. We moved in to one and rented the other seven. My payments were $522 a month and we were doing fairly good, with a nice income. By that time I was working again in my old gas station. James Lippertz was running it and it wasn't doing too good. After I was there a few months, it picked up again.

Retirement

By the summer of 1965, I was 65 years old and wanted to retire. I told my wife that I was retiring from the gas station and for her to take it easy. I would manage the apartments. She wanted to sell and get out. She was not getting along with some of the tenants; she had nothing to do with them. There were a lot of vacancies in the county of Santa Clara then.

So, we sold the whole thing and made only $10,000. Another big mistake we made, this was a lulu.

We moved back to the Valley and bought five acres of wine grapes for $15,000 and had a builder build us a three bedroom house with three baths for $13,500. Today that house is worth $100,000. We lived there 7 years doing very good. Then my wife got restless again. She was not getting along with one of the neighbors. We had the place fixed up real nice. So one day, she said, "Let's ask for a good price people will not pay. We asked for $45,500 and the first people to hear of the sale bought it without question, and I also kept that year's crop of grapes.

Then we went to Modesto, California and bought a new house for $23,500. I had to borrow $8,000 from Bank of America; because, the fellow that bought the ranch only gave us a $15,500 down payment and the remaining $30,000 balance at 7% interest.

When I harvested the grapes that fall of 1972, I paid the bank half of the loan. By 1973, I finished paying the bank loan. We spent $2,000 in the new home – new rugs, drapes and landscape. It was a nice house. We loved it very much. In the summer it was rather hot. I didn't mind; but, my wife didn't like the climate.

We had some nice friends in Modesto and were happy there. We visited each other and had a nice garden with fruits and vegetables growing all over the place.

By that time, my daughter Mary bought an old house in San Jose, California. It was real bad. She hired a carpenter and had the kitchen done over. Once in a while we visit her.

By July 1976, my wife began to get restless again. She was not getting along with her brother, Tony so she began to complain about the weather, it was too hot.

About the same time, Carmen Diaz was visiting us in Modesto and told my wife how much she liked living in a mobile home. We had visited her a few times before and my wife liked the mobile home. I did not care too much for it. To keep the peace in the family, we sold our house in Modesto and came here to Casa de Amigos Park and bought a mobile home for $24,000. We have landscaped the yard and it looks much better, but the rent has been increasing every year and it is getting unbearable.

In the spring of 1978, she began to get restless again and we started to look for an old house in old Sunnyvale, but there was none to be had except old junk that they were asking $65,000 for. I told my wife, "This is it. We are staying in the mobile park, come what may."

Of course, we have some nice friends here in the park and outside also.

By the way, we also joined the Senior Citizen Club in Sunnyvale, California. We go there when she feels good and see some of our old friends. She had a stroke about two years ago and some days she feels bad. That is why I go along with her she does not get excited and nervous.

This week we had a 4th of July celebration of 1978. A Spanish lady in the park had sewed the American flag in all embroidery. It was beautiful. The lady got the first prize. Two men playing the Spanish guitar got second prize and the ladies dancing Spanish got third.

So this is the high lights of my life up to August 1978. I know I misspell some words, but what is to be expected from a 7 year old immigrant that went to the 6th grade in grammar school in this country.

I could have written all of this in the Spanish language, but my grandchildren do not speak Spanish, so I did the best I could in English.

CUBA

In 1896, my father, Manuel Lopez Bilbao, was drafted into the military service in Spain. He was taken to San Roque, Spain, by the rock of Gibraltar, in a training camp there.

He was given the overseas shots that were required for service overseas. One day they were practicing shooting with a single shot rifle, an old fashion gun. He never fired a gun in his life. It kicked him so bad, he went down. His arms were swollen from the shots. The sergeant got hell for making him practice in that condition.

After that he was shipped to Cuba, after he learned how to shoot. He served under the Spanish general, Weyler (the Spanish Butcher). The reason for that name was that he was a new commander in the island. He wanted to stop the rebellion in Cuba, so he posted signs over the island saying nothing would happen if they give up fighting and come to the towns peacefully and he gave them three months to do it. By the end of three months, only women and children came in. The men kept on fighting, so he gave his soldiers orders to finish up with the men, clean up the island. First they went to provincia (province) of pinar del Rio, west of Havana, then they went to the provincial of Santa Clara, east of Havana.

In the meantime, (Wall Street) wanted the sugar and tobacco industry in the island. It was not the American government.

The Spanish would not give up the island, so the American government sent its fleet to the coastal waters. At the same time the battleship Maine was in Havana Bay. So one night at 9 p.m. there was a loud explosion in the bay. There were no shots fired from Morro Fort. The Maine went down with over 200 sailors killed.

Years later, the American government brought the Maine up from the bottom of the bay and it showed the steel plates of the ship were blown from the inside out. The American government sent an apology to the Spanish government.

The American fleet grouped together near Santiago do Cuba, they had eleven battleships, all had sixteen inch guns including the battleship Oregon.

The Spanish fleet consisted of five small battleships with six inch guns. To the battle started, the Spanish guns could not reach the American ships.

The American navy picked the Spanish ships like shooting fish in a barrel. They sank for and one escaped to Santiago bay. There the Spanish soldiers sank it in the channel. The sailors swam to shore and the Cuban rebels chopped them down with machetes.

A few days later the American troops landed near Santiago bay. That is where Ted Roosevelt brought his rough riders to San Juan Hill. Most of them were from the southwest, especially from New Mexico and Texas. The government promised them a horse and one hundred dollars bonus. They got the horse, but no hundred dollars.

So up they went to San Juan Hill. There were two Spanish Army companies on top of the hill. They had the yellow fever and were resting from the heat.

Up came the Rough Riders in full force, the Spanish soldiers had better fire arms, they had the German Mauser.

Finally the American forces overwhelmed them by force. In the Philippines the American fleet did the same thing.

The Spanish Army never gave up their firearms of any kind. A few German war ships took the Spanish forces back to Spain. One of the ships went to Málaga. My father was on it. It was December 24, 1898. The troops nearly froze to death. There they gave up their firearms in the bullring. When my father and the rest of the soldiers asked for their bonus pay, they were turned down. Finally, after a lot of argument, the government paid them what was theirs.

NOTE by Susan Burkholder in 2020. This is my grandfather's perspective in 1978, largely attributed to what he learned from his father's perspective from the late 1800's and early 1900's. Neither of my predecessors were trained historians. They simply shared their experiences, which may often be more accurate in historical perspective than those of distant "historians".

1966 Garden

How to Make
Spanish Style Olives

First, pick the olives when they get straw colored or just before they start to get black. Get a sharp knife and cut the olive 2-3 times, depends on the size olive. Make cut deep to the pit. Put the olives in a crock, 4 or 5 gallon size. It takes about 2 gallons of water to fill up to 2 inches from the (top).

To each gallon of water, put one cup of all-purpose salt or ½ pint of salt. Which is the same. To this same water add the same amount of vinegar, 2 heads of garlic and a small handful of oregano.

Do this when olives are sweet which will take about 4 weeks to sweeten.

After all the spices are in the crock for two weeks, they are ready to eat or put in jars. They will last for years.

José carried on his Andalucían heritage of raising varied crops. I wish I had a photo of him with his olive trees.

1969 Cucumber

1970 Fruit Tree

1986 Grapes

Joseph Lopez with his son (Tony) and his youngest daughter (Jo/Josie).

1955: The Lopez women and the first born grandchild of Joseph Lopez (Steve): L to R: Vi, (LaVida Davis) married Tony Lopez; Jo (Josie, Josephine); Steve Gass (Mary's son); Josie (Josefa/Josephine); Mary (Steve's mother)

1963: Joseph Lopez, Gary Gass, Susan Hassinger, Josie Lopez, Michael Lopez, Ronnie Lopez, Jerry Hassinger, Tony Lopez, Jr. Missing: Teri Lopez, Lynnette Lopez, Steve Gass

Borrego Sisters at the 1964 wedding of Connie's son
Josefa Lopez (Josie, Josephine), Teresa Segura (Teresa Ruiz), Connie Campoy
(Incarnacion/Carnation)

Joseph and Josephine Lopez on their 62nd anniversary

Lopezes mark 62 years of marriage

Josephine Borrego Lopez and Joseph Lopez of Woodland recently celebrated their 62nd wedding anniversary with family and friends.

The celebration, which was

ANNIVERSARY

held at St. John's Retirement Home, took the form of a luncheon attended by fellow residents and staff.

A blue and white cake was served at the luncheon.

Josephine, who was born July 1, 1911, in Seville, Spain, and Joseph, who was born April 9, 1900, in Granada, Spain, met when they were neighbors in Chico.

They were married Jan. 27, 1927, in Roseville.

The couple have three children, Mary Gass of San Jose, Tony Lopez of Los Gatos, and Josephine Hassinger of San Antonio, Texas.

Geneology

Parents, Grandparents and Siblings of Joseph LOPEZ Lopez		
From the Lopez memoirs and Ancestry.com		
José RAMON Lopez		
B: 1850 Spain		
D: 1989: Spain	**Manuel LOPEZ Bilbao**	
	B: February 1876: Spain	
	D: August 1945 California	
Maria BILBAO Alvarez		
B: 1852: Spain		
D: 1903:Spain		**Joseph LOPEZ Lopez**
		José, Joe
		B: April 10, 1900: Izbor, Spain
		D: November 11, 1993: California
		Siblings of Joseph LOPEZ Lopez
		Delores (Laura) LOPEZ Lopez
		B: Approx. 1902 Izbor, Spain
Antonio LOPEZ Lopez		*Married Name: Lozano*
B: 1852: Spain		*Antonia (Rose) LOPEZ Lopez*
D: 1918 Spain	**Maria (Marie) LOPEZ Diaz**	*B: August 1907 Hilo, Hawai'I*
	B: March 1877: Spain	*Manuel LOPEZ Lopez*
Maria de Cruz DIAZ Lopez	D: July 1957: California	*B: February 1916 California*
B: 1854: Spain		*D: August 1916 California*
D: 1936: Spain		*Mary LOPEZ Lopez*
		B: April 1913: California
		Married Name: Rios
		Frank LOPEZ Lopez
		B: Jan 1919: California

Children and Descendants of Joseph LOPEZ Lopez and Josefa (Josephine) BORREGO Lopez

Children	Grandchildren	Great Grandchildren
Mary Braun B: 1927	Steve B: 1948	
Married Art Gass	Gary B: 1962	
Married Bob Braun		
Tony Lopez B: 1929	Tony B:1955	Antonio Borrego Lopez III
Married LaVida Davis	Ronald B: 1957	Caprice
	Teri B: 1959	Jennifer
	Lynnette B: 1960	
	Michael B: 1962	
Josephine Hassinger B:1932	Gerald B:1959	Megan
Married Russell Neal Hassinger	Susan B: 1962	

Siblings and their families of Manuel LOPEZ Bilbao (Aunts/Uncles/Cousins of Joseph LOPEZ Lopez)

From the ship manifest of the Heliopolis and the Lopez memoirs:
All listed except Patricio were on the Heliopolis. More cousins may have been born in Hawai'i and California.
Birth years are approximated based on age from the Heliopolis manifest

Patricio LOPEZ Bilbao: Did not leave Spain on the Heliopolis. Went to war and settled in Ceuta.	
Ana LOPEZ Bilbao B: 1867	
Husband: Antonio SALAZAR Molina B: 1865	
	Children:
	Maria Josefa SALAZAR Lopez B: 1889
	Antonio SALAZAR Lopez B: 1894
	Francesca SALAZAR Lopez B: 1900
	Ana SALAZAR Lopez B: 1904
	Juan SALAZAR Lopez B: 1906
Juan LOPEZ Bilbao B: 1873	
Wife: Antonia SALAZAR Rodriguez B: 1876	
	Children:
	Antonio LOPEZ Salazar B: 1897
	José LOPEZ Salazar B: 1899
	Juan LOPEZ Salazar B: 1905
Antonio LOPEZ Bilbao B: 1870	
Wife: Maria Exposito B: 1876	
	Children:
	Eduardo LOPEZ Exposito B: 1898
	Manuel LOPEZ Exposito B: 1902
	Antonio LOPEZ Exposito B: 1905

Parents and Grandparents of Josefa BORREGO Perez (Wife of Joseph LOPEZ Lopez)

From the ship manifests of the Harpalion, Willesden, the Lopez memoirs, Ancestry.com, and family records

Antonio BORREGO Bernal		
B: Montellano, Spain		
	Antonio BORREGO Romero	
	B: Approx. 1879 Montellano, Spain	
	To Hawai'i via Harpalion 1912	
	D: 1931: California	
Conception ROMERO Gordo		
B: Montellano, Spain		
		Josefa BORREGO Perez
		Josephine, Josie
		B: July 10, 1911: Montellano Spain
		To Hawai'i via Harpalion 1912
José PEREZ Lopez		D: 1996: Round Rock, Texas
B: Feb 1856 Montellano, Spain		
To Hawai'i via Willesden 1913		
D: 1941 California		
	Manuela "Emma" PEREZ Romero	
	B: February 1884 Montellano, Spain	
	To Hawai'i via Harpalion 1912	
	D 1960: California	
Teresa ROMERO Tecero		
B: 1862 Montellano, Spain		
To Hawai'i via Willesden 1913		
D: 1942 California		

Other Children of José PEREZ Lopez and Teresa ROMERO Tecero Aunts and Uncles of Josefa BORREGO Perez

Joseph (José) PEREZ Romero To Hawai'i via Harpalion 1912	B: 1883 Montellano, Spain	D: 1919 San Francisco , CA of "Flu" (source: memoirs)
Juan or Manuel PEREZ Romero To Hawai'i via Willesden 1913	B: 1892 Montellano, Spain	D: 1959 Oakland, CA
Diego Perez Romero To Hawai'i via Willesden 1913	B: 1896 (Ancestry.com) (Willesden manifest: incorrect age) Montellano, Spain	D: 1969 Fairfield, CA

Siblings and their families of Josefa BORREGO Perez
(Wife of Joseph LOPEZ Lopez)

From the ship manifests of the Harpalion, the Lopez memoirs, Ancestry.com, and family records

Antonio (Tony) BORREGO Perez	Son: Antonio Borrego Daughters: Mildred (Millie) and Catherine	
B: 1906 Montellano, Spain	To Hawai'i via Harpalion 1912	
D: 1987 California		
Wife: Isabelle Mena B: 1910 Cadiz, Spain D: 2000 California		
Teresa BORREGO Perez	Son: John Ruiz Daughters: Presentación Maria Ruiz McAlister (PR/Mary) ManuelaRuiz Miller (Emma)	Grandchildren: Linda McAlister Modar, James McAlister, Jr. Laura Miller Clarke, Mark Miller Great Grandchildren: Lisa, Craig, James, Danny, Jaimie, Maria, Robert
B: January 1907 Montellano, Spain	To Hawai'i via Harpalion 1912	
D: 1991 California		
Husband 1: Antonio Ruiz		
Husband 2: José Segura (M:1956)		
Maria BORREGO Perez	Only record of Maria's given name is the manifest for the Harpalion.	
B: 1909 (?) Montellano, Spain		
D: 1912 on Board the Harpalion		
Josefa (Josephine, Josie) BORREGO Perez	Wife of Joseph LOPEZ Lopez: Details for her descendants on p. 59	
B: July 10, 1911: Montellano Spain	To Hawai'i via Harpalion 1912	
D: 1996: Round Rock, Texas		
Incarnacion (Connie/Carnation) BORREGO Perez	Sons: Dennis and Frank Campoy	Granddaughters: Lisa, Kathryn Ann, Christina Louise, Cari Sue.
B: February, 16, 1916 Waipahu, Hawai'i		
D: November 8, 2004 Husband: Frank Campoy		
Joseph (Joe) BORREGO Perez		
B: 1917: Hawai'i		
D: 1935: California		
A brother (**Manuel**) and sister (**Mary**) were born in Hawai'i and died in Hawai'i.		
Ralph BORREGO Perez		
B: 1922 California		
D: ?		
Wife: Doris		
John BORREGO Perez		
B 1924: California		
D: ?		
Two Marriages		

Partial Ship Manifests

1912 Harpalion & 1913 Willesden
for the family of
Josefa BORREGO Perez; Jose Lopez Lopez's wife

Harpalion

Departure February, 1912. Arrival in Hawaii April, 1912

Josefa at 9 months; her parents; brother and two sisters;

and her maternal uncle, José PEREZ Romero.

Ship	Image	Page	Line	Surname	Name	Age	Sex	Status	Residence in Spain	Province	Birthplace	Err
4-Harpalion			23	Borrego Romero	Antonio	33	M	M	Montellano (Sevilla)	Sevilla	Montellano (Sevilla)	Y
4-Harpalion			24	Perez Romero	Manuela	26	F	M	Montellano (Sevilla)	Sevilla	Montellano (Sevilla)	Y
4-Harpalion			25	Borrego Perez	Antonio	6	M	S	Montellano (Sevilla)	Sevilla	Montellano (Sevilla)	Y
4-Harpalion			26	Borrego Perez	Teresa	5	F	S	Montellano (Sevilla)	Sevilla	Montellano (Sevilla)	Y
4-Harpalion			27	Borrego Perez	Maria	2	F	S	Montellano (Sevilla)	Sevilla	Montellano (Sevilla)	Y
4-Harpalion			28	Borrego Perez	Josefa	9mo	F	S	Montellano (Sevilla)	Sevilla	Montellano (Sevilla)	Y
4-Harpalion			29	Perez Romero	Jose	29	M	S	Montellano (Sevilla)	Sevilla	Montellano (Sevilla)	Y
4-Harpalion			30	Barón Antero	Rufino	43	M	M	Puente del Concejo (Salamanca)	Salamanca	Puente del Concejo (Salamanca)	Y

Willesden 1913

Second Trip from Spain to Hawaii

Departure February, 1913. Arrival in Hawaii March, 1913.

Josefa's maternal grandparents and two uncles

Family records have Manuel's name as Juan.

Ancestry.com documents show Diego's birth as 1896. He was 17 in 1913, not 4.

Ship	Image	Page	Line	Surname	Name	Age	Sex	Status	Residence in Spain	Province	Birthplace	Err
5-Willesden		1449	11	Perez Lopez	Jose	52	M	M	Montellano (Sevilla)	Sevilla	Montellano (Sevilla)	Y
5-Willesden		1449	12	Romero Tercero	Teresa	46	F	M	Montellano (Sevilla)	Sevilla	Montellano (Sevilla)	Y
5-Willesden		1449	13	Perez Romero	Manuel	21	M	S	Montellano (Sevilla)	Sevilla	Montellano (Sevilla)	Y
5-Willesden		1449	14	Perez Romero	Diego	4	M	S	Montellano (Sevilla)	Sevilla	Montellano (Sevilla)	Y

Family Documents

Certificate of Baptism for Josefa BORREGO Perez

Certificate of Birth of Josefa BORREGO Perez

Serie AC № 205009

MINISTERIO DE JUSTICIA
Registros Civiles

CERTIFICACION LITERAL DE INSCRIPCION DE Nacimiento —— (1)

Sección Primera
Tomo 48 —
Pág. — — —
Folio (2) 2 — —

REGISTRO CIVIL DE Montellano — — —
Provincia de Sevilla — — — —

El asiento al margen reseñado literalmente dice así: En la villa de Montellano, á las once del día trece de Julio de mil novecientos once, ante D. Rafael Corbacho Romero, Juez Municipal y D. Rafael Alvarez Gallardo, Suplente Secretario, compareció D. ANTONIO BORREGO ROMERO, natural de esta villa, termino municipal de iden provincia de Sevilla, de edad de treinta y dos años, de estado casado, su ejercicio del campo, domiciliado en esta villa, calle, Canova del Castillo, según acredita por cédula personal que exhebe, solicitando que se inscriba en el Registro Civil, una niña, y al efecto como padre de la misma declaró: Que dicha niña, nació en la casa del declarante el día diez del corriente mes á las nueve de la mañana: Que es hija legitima del declarante y de su mujer MANUELA PEREZ ROMERO, natural de esta villa, termino municipal del iden provincia de Sevilla, de edad de veintisiete años, dedicada á las ocupaciones propia de su sexo y domiciliada en el de su marido: Que es nieta por linea paterna de D. Antonio Borrego Bernal, natural de esta villa, provincia de Sevilla, mayor de edad y domiciliado en esta villa y de Dª. Concepcion Romero Gordo, natural de esta villa, provincia de Sevilla, mayores de edad y domiciliada con su marido, y por linea materna de D. Jose Perez Lopez, natural de esta villa, provincia de Sevilla, mayor de edad, casado, y de Dª. Teresa Romero Tercero, naturalde esta villa, provincia de Sevilla, mayor de edad, casada y domiciliada con su marido: Y que expresada niña se le ha puesto el nombre de JOSEFA.- Todo ásto presenciaron como

testigos D. Jose Diaz Jimenez y D. Francisco Palma
Avendaño, ambos naturales de esta villa, mayores
de edad, casados, empleados y domiciliado en esta
villa.- Leida integramente esta acta, ó invitadas
las personas que deben suscribirla á que la leyeran
por si mismas su asi lo creian conveniente, se es-
tampó en ella el sello del Registro Civil y la firmaro
el Sr. Juez los testigos presenciales y por el com-
parecelate que no sabe lo hace Jose Diaz Jimenez,
de esta vecindad y de todo ello como Secretario Suplente certifico.= Rafael Corbacho.= Jose Diaz.=
Francisco Palma.= Rafael Alverez=: Rubricado y se-
llado.- Lo copiado concuerda con su original a que
me remito.

(Sello del Registro Civil)

CERTIFICA: *Según consta de la página registral reseñada al margen, el*
Encargado D. Antonio Gil Guerrero — — — —

Montellano, a 18 de Abril de 19 73

(En los Juzgados de Paz, firmarán el Juez y el Secretario)

Importe de la certificación:

Tarifa Tributaria, n.º 32 (en pólizas).... 5,00 ptas.
Tasas (Decretos de 18-6-59, art. 4, y ar-
 ticulo 37, tarifa 1.ª)................ 32,00 »
Busca (art. 40, tarifa 1.ª) (3)........... .... »
Urgencia (art. 41, tarifa 1.ª) (4)....... .... »
Impreso (5)........................... 13,00 »
 TOTAL............... ....

Translation of the birth certificate by Luis Arizpe

MINISTRY OF JUSTICE
Civil Registry

FACTUAL REGISTRATION CERTIFICATE OF BIRTH
Civil Registry of Montellano
Province of Sevilla

The person seated says, word for word:

In the villa (town) of Montellano, at 11 a.m. on the 13th of July, 1911, before Don ("D.") Rafael Corbacho Romero, Municipal Judge and Don ("D.") Rafael Alvarez Gallardo, Alternate Secretary, arraigned D.Antonio Borrego Romero, native of this villa, this municipal term of said province, Sevilla, being of 32 years of age, married, trained of field (ranch hand), domiciled in this villa, on Canova del Castillo St, according to accredited identity card(s),soliciting an inscription (registration) in the Civil Registry, a girl, and being the father of the child declares: That this child, born in the above house on the 10th the current month a 9 a.m.: That she is the legitimate child of his wife Manuela Perez Romero, native of this villa, this municipal term of said province, Sevilla, being of 27 years of age, being occupied in the proper occupations of her sex (housewife) and living with her husband: That she (baby girl) is grandchild in the paternal lineage of D. Antonio Borrego Bernal, native of this villa, province of Sevilla, senior of age and domiciled in this villa and of Doña ("Da.") Conception Romero Gordo, native of this villa, province of Sevilla, senior of age and domiciled with her husband, and of the maternal lineage of D. José Perez Lopez, native of this villa, province of Sevilla, senior of age, married, and of Da.Teresa Romero Tercero, native of this villa, province of Sevilla, senior of age, married and living with her husband: And that they have named the newly birthed girl Josefa - All this was presented to witnesses D. José Diaz Jimenez and D. Fransicsco Palma Avendaño, both native of this villa, aged in years, married, employed and domiciled in this villa. — Read with integrity this act, and invited (asked) the persons that they should read it for themselves so that they should both affirm it's truthfulness, it was stamped with the seal of the Civil Registry and signed by the Judge in the presence of the witnesses (face to face) and it appeared that he who doesn't know doesn't do (so help them) José Diaz Jimenez, of this neighborhood et al. as the certified Alternate Secretary. = Rafael Alvarez = Endorsed and sealed (stamped). — It was copied in accordance with the original that was referred to me.

Certified: According to the registration page copied in the margin:

The Person in Charge D. Antonio Gil Guerrero
Montellano, the 18th of April, 1973.

Location of the Lopez and Borrego Families in Hawaii

Compiled via research by Susan Burkholder

As per Joseph Lopez Lopez's memoirs, the Lopez family worked on the island of Hawaii. Via my grandfather's story of walking three miles to the Catholic school, I learned that the plantation they worked was near Hilo.

Also from the memoirs it is clear that all six of the families from Izbor lived at Hamaulo Camp Number 4, near Hilo, Hawaii. Seven families left Izbor, one family did not board in Malaga due to a suspected illness from one of the family members having "red eyes."

It was unclear to me until recently where in Hawaii my grandmother's family (BORREGO Perez) worked after coming over on the Harpalion in 1912 and the Willesden in 1913.

Yet, in researching my grandmother's siblings; I learned that my great-aunt Connie (my mother's favorite aunt); Incarnacion BORREGO Perez; was born in Waipahu, on the island of Oahu. Therefore, at least a portion of the BORREGO Perez family lived and worked in or near Waipahu, Oahu, Hawaii.

According to Wikipedia: https://en.wikipedia.org/wiki/Waipahu,_Hawaii:

> "**Waipahu** *is a former* sugarcane plantation *town.* ...*In 1897, Oahu Sugar Company was incorporated, and its board of directors located the sugar mill in Waipahu.* ...*each worker was assigned*

*a number inscribed on a metal disc about the size of a silver dollar. The numbers 1 through 899 identified Japanese alien; 900 through 1400 were Japanese who were American citizens or Hawaii-born. The 2000 and 2100 series were Portuguese laborers, **2200 Spanish**, 2300 Hawaiian, 2400 Puerto Rican, 3000 Chinese or Korean, 4000 and 5000 Filipino aliens, and Filipino Americans. Each ethnic group was broken up into different camps."*

The memoirs provide limited information of when the BORREGO Perez side of my family came to California. Documents seem to show that some came to California earlier than others. They are first mentioned in the memoirs in 1917, when Joseph Lopez Lopez meets José Perez Romero (Josefa's uncle.) Family records show that John Borrego Perez (Josefa's younger brother) was born in 1917 in Hawaii. Ancestry.com immigration records show that Diego Perez Romero (another of Josefa's uncles) immigrated to California in November of 1919.

Alphabetical List: Family and Friends

Alphabetical List **FRIENDS and FAMILY of Joseph Lopez Lopez** **(For descendants to find their Spanish forbearers)**		
Last	**First**	
Borrego	Antonio	Father-in-law of José Lopez. Married to Manuela Perez Romero.
Borrego, Campoy	Connie (Incarnacion) Married Name: Campoy	Sister of Josephine Borrego Perez. Sister-in-law of José Lopez. Married Frank Campoy.
Borrego	Josephine (Josefa) , Josie	Josefa Borrego Perez. Wife of José Lopez. Daughter of Manuela Perez Romero and Antonio Borrego Romero.
Borrego	Tony (Antonio)	Brother of Josephine Borrego Perez. Brother-in-law of José Lopez. Co-owned Gas station with José Lopez
Calvo	Emily (Emilia) Maiden Name Lozano.	Lived near the schoolhouse in Camp 4. Her cousin was the Yolo County Supervisor in 1978
Cano	Antonio	Worked in a hops ranch north of Hopland, California in 1914. Argued their case to the District Attorney.
Cano	Philip	Worked in a hops ranch north of Hopland, California in 1914. Argued their case to the District Attorney.
Diaz	Carmen	Arrived on the Heliopolis. Was not in Camp 4; but was on Hawaii Island ("The Big Island"). Friend of Josephine Lopez
Diaz	Joe	Witness for José Lopez's registration to become a citizen. Cousin exchanged money for the 1949 Spain Trip.

Alphabetical List FRIENDS and FAMILY of Joseph Lopez Lopez (For descendants to find their Spanish forbearers)		
Escano	Edward (Eduardo)	Friend of José Lopez
Escano	Mr. Escano Sr.	Father of Tony and Edward (Eduardo). Bought Manuel Lopez Bilbao's land and horses in Hawaii.
Escano	Tony	Friend of José Lopez
Espigares	Joe	Uncle of Emilia (Emily) Calvo (née Lozano). Lived near the schoolhouse in Camp 4.
Flores	José	Friend of José Lopez. Wife, Mary, was cousin to Josephine Galiano.
Galiano	José	Worked in the railroad depot in Chico, CA
Galiano	Josephine	Born in Melilla, Spanish Morocco. Came to Hawaii on the Heliopolis. Married Joe Guzman. Lived in Hayward, CA.
Gallardo	Manuel	Friend of José Lopez.
Gallardo	Ralph	Friend of José Lopez. Married Virginia Romero.
Gass, Braun	Mary	José Lopez's first daughter. Born in 1927. Married Art Gass: Two sons, Steve and Gary. Later Married Bob Braun.
Gonzales	Joe	Served as witness for José Lopez's registration to become a citizen.
Guerrero	Antonio	Gave Manuel Lopez Bilbao a job. Children: Valverde and Bravo. Harvested grapes and prunes in Geyersville.
Guzman	Joe	Married Josephine Galiano. Lived in Hayward, CA
Hassinger	Josephine, Jo, Josie	José Lopez's second daughter. Born in 1932. Married Russell Neal Hassinger. Two children: Gerald (Jerry) and Susan.
Hassinger	Russell Neal	Married Josephine Lopez, José's second daughter.
Lippertz	Marina	Born on the Heliopolis. Lived in Mountain View in 1978

		Alphabetical List FRIENDS and FAMILY of Joseph Lopez Lopez (For descendants to find their Spanish forbearers)
Lopez	Antonia (Rose/Rosie)	José Lopez's second sister. First Spanish baby born in Camp 4.
Lopez	Frank	Brother of José Lopez. Served in WWII. Worked at the Libby Cannery through the late 1970's.
Lopez	Juan	Cousin to Manuel Lopez Bilbao.
Lopez	Laura (Delores)	José Lopez's oldest sister. Born in 1904. Married John Lozano in 1927.
Lopez	Mary	José Lopez's third sister. Born in 1913. Married name was Rios
Lopez	Tony	José Lopez's cousin.
Lopez	Tony	José Lopez's son. Born in 1929. Married LaVida Davis (Vi). Five children: Tony, Ronald, Teri, Lynette, Michael.
Lopez Chavez	Josefa	José Lopez's cousin in Izbor del Rio. José's granddaughter, Susan Burkholder, met Josefa's granddaughter, Encarus, in Izbor, Granada, Spain in 2017.
Lozano	Emily (Emilia) Married name: Calvo	Lived near the schoolhouse in Camp 4. Her cousin was the Yolo County Supervisor in 1978
Marquez	Belin	Lived in San Leandro. Died in an accident with her husband and others between San Leandro and San Francisco.
Marquez	John	Worked with José Lopez in the rice fields. He and his mother lived with the Lopez family. Died in 1972
Marquez	José (Pepe)	From Valdepeñas, Spain. Came to California with his uncle. Taught José Lopez Spanish. José taught him English. Married a Spaniard. Lived in Pittsburgh, CA. Died in 1972.
Morales	- family -	Came with the Lopez's from Spain. "Played a big part" in José' life.

Alphabetical List FRIENDS and FAMILY of Joseph Lopez Lopez (For descendants to find their Spanish forbearers)		
Morales	Frank	Lived in Rocklin, worked in New Castle. Helped José Lopez and Josephine Borrego Perez elope.
Moreno	Manuel	Schoolmate of José Lopez. Entrepreneur. Became a wealthy man in Sunnyvale.
Ojeda	Art	Distributed movie advertising in exchange for free passes with José Lopez and John Santaella.
Ojeda	Bert	Born on the Heliopolis. Lived in Mountain View in 1978.
Ojeda	Tony	Cut firewood in the town of Cloverdale, California with Manuel Lopez Bilbao.
Perez	John	Lived in Tracy in 1978. Came on the Heliopolis, but went to a different island in Hawaii.
Perez Romero	José (Joseph)	Uncle of Josephine Lopez (Borrego); José's wife. Died in 1919 from the flu (memoirs)
Romero	Aurora	Daughter of John Romero. Died in 1931 in a cannery incident.
Romero	Harold	Worked at the Tom Styles Ranch with the Borrego family.
Romero	John	Friend of José Lopez. First wife died of the flu in 1918.
Romero	Rose	Older sister of Harold Romero.
Romero	Virginia	She was still in Spain in 1915. Her father and Uncle José met the Lopez family in Chico. Married Ralph Gallardo.
Salazar	Anna	Cousin to José Lopez. Worked in the Sebastopol apricot cannery.
Santaella	Chris	Lived on Third Street in Santa Rosa.
Santaella	Joe	Joe lived in Sunnyvale, California in 1978. He was head foreman in Libby's cannery.
Santaella	John	Distributed movie advertising in exchange for free passes with José Lopez and Art Ojeda.

Joseph Lopez Lopez (José)

His life, his family, his friends, and his memories.

Con mucho amor.

If you found José's memoirs to be of interest, please consider writing a review, posting or sharing your thoughts on Amazon, Ancestry. com or Facebook.

Your review, post, or share will help others to find José's story and experience his journey from Spain to Hawaii to California. Perhaps others will find their families in these pages.

Facebook Pages or Groups that may be of interest:
Hawaiian Spaniards
Andalucíans in California
Traces of Spanish Immigrants

We may be related if your forbearers were from Izbor, Granada, Spain: *Lopez, Bilbao, Lozano, Rios, Salazar*; or from Montellano, Sevilla, Spain: *Borrego, Romero, Perez, Tercero*

or

perhaps we are related by marriage, or simply from the connection of being descendants of Hawaiian Spaniards or any Spaniard.

I would love to hear from you and trace back how we are related: by friendship, marriage, bloodline, or just being Spaniards.

Susan Marie (Hassinger Lopez) Burkholder can be reached at JoseLopezMemoirs@gmail.com

Lightning Source UK Ltd.
Milton Keynes UK
UKHW021006051220
374628UK00012B/815